AF528021

"DAMSELS OF THE BAY"

(LATEST RESEARCHES AND EXPERIENCES ON ANDAMAN NICOBAR ISLANDS)

"DAMSELS OF THE BAY"

(LATEST RESEARCHES AND EXPERIENCES ON ANDAMAN NICOBAR ISLANDS)

Jai Prakash Mishra

RAJESH PUBLICATIONS

NEW DELHI - 110 002

ISBN : 81-85891-94-X

Published by :
M. L. Gupta
Rajesh Publications
1, Ansari Road, Darya Ganj,
New Delhi - 110 002

Typesetting by :
Anoop Arora
New Delhi-110 092

Printed in India at :
Jaico Printers, Darya Ganj,
New Delhi - 110 002

© Jai Prakash Mishra

First Published in India 2013

Price : Rs. 500.00

All rights Reserved with the Publisher including to translate or to reproduce this book parts of except for brief quotations in critical articles or reviews.

In
Loving Memory
of

Karttik Mishra

I.I.M. Shillong

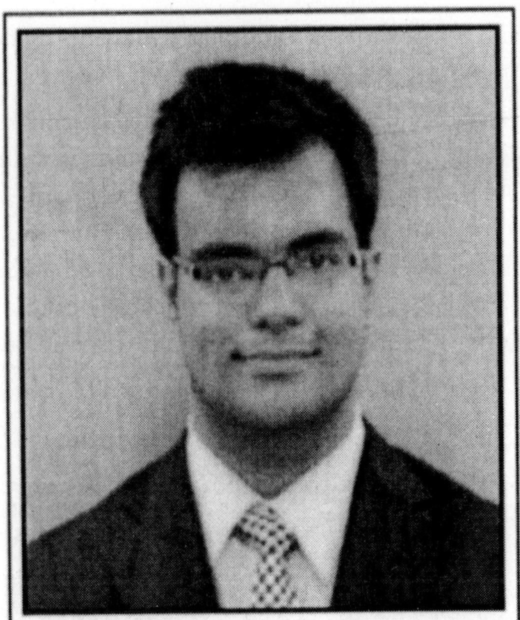

(27.11.1998 - 17.03.2013)

Dedicated
to

Sher Ali

(the unsung freedom fighter of Indian National Movement who preferred the gallows in Andaman to a life of servility under the imperialist power)

Ranjit Sinha
DIRECTOR

CENTRAL BUREAU OF INVESTIGATION
GOVERNMENT OF INDIA
5-B, C.G.O. COMPLEX,
LODHI ROAD,
NEW DELHI-110003

D. O. No. DPDRC/2013/048

Dated 05-04-2013

MESSAGE

I am glad to know that Shri J.P. Mishra has written this book on Andaman which covers the story of Andaman ever since it came to limelight because of the efforts of the British Army. This book is an attempt to present the valuable and informative materials about the people of Andaman, its Flora & Fauna the aboriginal tribes vis-à-vis the horrors created by the British in the Cellular Jail to demoralize the freedom fighters. Shri J.P. Mishra has served in these islands for two years and compiled his memories about the people who are living here in the lap of nature. The materials inside the book also defy the misnomer that Andaman is 'Kala Pani'.

It is hoped that the readers will know the true facts about these islands and understand the historical significance of Andaman in the freedom struggle. This book will be useful for the public servants, tourists and the researchers as well.

I bless J.P. for this endeavour.

05/04/13

(RANJIT SINHA)

New Delhi

Javeed Ahmad, IPS
Joint Director & HOZ

केन्द्रीय अन्वेषण ब्यूरो
CENTRAL BUREAU OF INVESTIGATION
भारत सरकार
GOVERNMENT OF INDIA
कार्यलय सयुक्त निदेशक
OFFICE OF THE JOINT DIRECTOR
डा. एस. के. सिंह पथ, बेली रोड
DR. S. K. SINGH PATH BAILEY ROAD
पटना - 800 022
PATNA - 800 022

Shri J.P. Mishra or simply 'JP' was always known to us as a professional police officer. He has now come up with his 'tribute' to the people of Andaman Islands and exposed a totally unknown side of his personality to us all and we are the richer for it.

Andaman Islands are today a popular tourist destination for many Indians and an increasing number of foreigners. The beauty of the Islands is well documented but Shri Mishra has now opened up before us aspects of its history, its people and interesting anecdotal insights about the original inhabitants of these Islands. The struggle of the Andaman people against the British must be recognised and celebrated by the rest of the country. The patriotic Sher Ali who preferred the gallows to a life of servility under the imperialist power is a model and inspiration for the new generation. The traditional knowledge of the tribes about their flora and fauna can be a starting point for many modern researchers. Surely this book will be a valuable and welcome addition to the writing about the Andaman Islands. J.P. has shown his creative side to us and demonstrated that an investigator's eye for detail can be great tool for a writer.

(Javeed Ahmad)

शक्ति सिन्हा
Shakti Sinha
मुख्य सचिव
Chief Secretary

अण्डमान तथा निकोबार प्रशासन
ANDAMAN AND NICOBAR ADMINISTRATION
सचिवालय SECRETARIAT
Port Blair, dated the 14th March, 2012

FOREWORD

Andaman - the name itself is synonymous with Kala Pani, surrounded by dark, deep sea, with the islands themselves epitomising breathtaking natural beauty. Shri Jai Prakash Mishra, a police officer who has been posted in Andaman Islands presents his book "**Damsels of the Bay**", which deserves a special place in the collective consciousness of country since it brings out many unique aspects of these islands. His experiences of the Andaman & Nicobar Islands have obviously moved him very much. He tries to put into words these unique aspects of these islands with he aims to familiarise the reader with them. Shri Mishra had the opportunity to study these islands closely during his posting and has understood these multiple dimensions very well. The book has depicted not only visual delights of the islands but it also excites the mind and imagination and also touches the heart. As one roads the book one feels that the author has actually 'experienced' both mental exhilaration and emotional delight, which he has tried to convey to the reader.

The chapter "**The Journey in the Offing**" deals with the feelings of a public servant who is asked to serve, at short notice, in this remote area in public interest. The effects of the posting, the planning of journey etc. has been well described in this chapter. The next chapter deals with the description of the life of the people, the flora and fauna and his interaction with the local officers as well as with the person on the street. The third chapter **"Andaman Tribals"** deals with the world's perception of the tribes of these islands and the picture as seen by Shri Mishra. **"The Making of the Cellular Jail"** describes in a very exciting way how colonisers felt the need to shift the prisoners from mainland India to this place, describing how the concept of Cellular Jail emerged and the story behind its construction. The following chapter is a very interesting read. It gives a vivid picture of Shri Mishra's interaction with the **freedom fighters,** who are alive at present. The author gives due importance to the less known facts about them. **"Lest we Forget"** deals with common lifestyle of the people living in Andaman and showcases the natural and sustainable ways they spend their lives. The Tsunami which created havoc years ago had also had a big bearing on the Andamans. The author elaborates on the rehabilitation and development works in the Islands and how the people recovered from the worst disaster the islands faced in living memory. He has described in a very objective manner how the political and administrative framework carried on after the disaster struck. The inclusion of Appendices which contains interesting information related to the Andamans, its flora and fauna would be helpful to researchers and specialists in the field to build upon.

I congratulate the author on this exceptional and thought-provoking work, which, I am sure, will be read with deep interest and profit.

(Shakti Sinha)

Panchanand Mishra
M.A. (Pat.) MA (U of Penna) Ph.D.(Bhu.u)
Chairman

Saraswati Sadan,
Swami Vivekanand Road,
Adampur, Bhagalpur
Bihar - 812 001

FOREWORD

I salute the indomitable spirit of the young officer of the C.B.I. who regarded his most anguishing transfer to the far off islands of Andaman and Nicobar as a blessing in disguise. Far away from his home town Patna to an unknown place which had been regarded as a Kala Pani because of the brutal treatment meted out to the freedom fighters by the British rulers, was inhabited by the tribals who were most unfriendly to outsiders. But the young officer wrote his first experience in Hindi as "Andaman Nahi Hai Kalapani". This is the English version of the above mentioned book which is more positive in outlook. Therefore, it has been justly entitled "Damsels of the Bay". The work reminds me of my conversation with Haribans Rai Bachchan in mid 60s at his residence at 4 Windsar Place at New Delhi. It course of our talk he mentioned that Jawaharlal Nehru asked him to translate his speech-English into Hindi. He did it and attached a note on it as "translation is like a lady-if faithful she is ugly and if beautiful she is unfaithful." Therefore, it is an unfaithful translation and hence it is "Damself of the Bay."

The book is more than a mere translation of the Hindi version. It has added more flesh and flavor intertwined with a rare style of adding an autobiography as well. It reminds me of a few words of Rudyard Kipling's epic poem "If"

"If you can dream-and not make dreams your master;
If you can think-and not make dreams your master;
If you can meet with Triumph and Disaster
And treat those two imposters just the same
....
Yours is the Earth; and everything that is in it

Panchanand Mishra

REMINISCENCES

I came to Andaman and Nicobar Islands as part of my official duties in November 2004. This was one month before the **devastating Tsunami** struck the Islands in December 2004.

Soon after my joining, **the entire Andaman and Nicobar Islands** went through a very devastating spell of natural calamities. Fortunately, I could contribute immensely to the relief and rehabilitation work in the Islands after the Tsunami.

In appreciation of my contribution to the **Islanders** through the medium of Doordarshan in the relief and rehabilitation work during and after the **Tsunami,** the Government of India and the Andaman and Nicobar Administration **conferred meritorious service to me** during the Republic Day celebrations in 2008.

Looking back, I can say that I had a very memorable tenure in Andaman and Nicobar Islands from 2004 to 2008.

I still fondly remember my association with friends like **K.P. Jayarajan, Dr. Thulasi** and **J.P. Mishra.** On many evenings, we used to get together and share our experiences in the **Islands**. During such meetings, I still remember that J.P. Mishraji was a fond listener and he used to gather much information from Dr. Thulasi and Jayarajan, who had very long and **distinctive service career in the Islands.**

I am extremely happy that Mishraji is **recycling and remoulding whatever he had gathered during his stint** in the Islands and is at present channeling these memories into unforgettable reading experience.

I wish him all success in his endeavors.

Trivandrum
KENDRA
16th April, 2012
KERALA

(P.K. SUBASH)
DEPUTY DIRECTOR GENERAL
DOORDARSHAN

TRIVANDRUM,

PREFACE

'Damsels of the Bay' is a fitting epitaph on Andaman. The Colonial rulers were in a comfortable position to use this phrase once upon a time when they invaded this country with an evil design. Playing with the waves of ocean and beautiful fountain emerging from the top of the hill may be a death trap also but it do not undermine the beauty of the nature as well. Your thoughts reflect your personality and this truly happened when these beautiful islands were considered for victimizing the prisoners struggling for their mother land. These places could have been developed as a wonderful tourist spot also. An Indian couple who met me in the Red skin Island was simply hypnotized by the beauty of the Islands "I have seen many parts of the world, but the beauty of this place is simply remarkable and praiseworthy."

If you have any evil design in your mind, you are going to be exposed sooner or later. It is against nature and hence unacceptable. This is true with the concept of 'Kala-Pani' - an adjective which was the brain child of the British – a bi-product of their prejudiced thought - a sense of false vanity of superiority complex. They wanted to let down the beauty of the Islands - the flora and fauna but their preconceived thoughts did not last long. They have gone, their thoughts were of no use and hence not adopted. Andaman is a destination of first choice for the Indians as well as the foreigner. A group of more than 500 islands in the Bay of Bengal pushes us back in the realm of fantasy and made us feel about these "dancing damsels of the Bay."

I wanted to meet the people of 'Kala-Pani.' My dream came true but with an unfortunate note. It was not a routine transfer and unexpected. It was issued in so called 'Public interest.' These two words are very dangerous for a public servant and permanent source of mental torture. I had a lot of apprehension for the people and the land I had to visit. At a time of distress, negative thoughts germinate in mind and I was not an exception. Before my departure, I got lots of feed back also. Ignoring all, I visited

Port-Blair and served there for almost two years as a Police Officer. The people living in these so called 'kala-pani' are undoubtedly better than the main landers, full of emotions and sentiments, they know how to love and care. Though they prefer to live in pomp and show but their intentions are not commercialized. Point of sentiment is still alive. One day my domestic help had told me "Officers from mainland used to come, we used to serve but after departure they forgot everything including us." I had assured this would not happen and he could trust me at least. The kind of love and affection, I got there compelled me to write about them and this book is nothing but a tribute to them – to the people and the land – a place which was enriched by the patriotic flavour of Veer Savarkar and many others who sacrificed everything for our survival. They will glitter in the annals of the History in the years to come slapping on the ugly face of colonizers, who resorted to crush their impregnable sentiments and sense of loyalty towards the mother land. I at the same time remember all my friends Grewal, Swamy, Doctor, Subas and many others who were the part of my journey during the so called days of asylum. An individual is good and bad and not the community. I was victimized by a group of persons but lots extended their helping hands also in the mainland and in the islands both. God has given us place to stand and survive and it is He only who can take it from us. He also does not tolerate any interference in that. A human being, if interferes in the law of the nature, he is bound to face the consequences. A victim, therefore, should not resort to any activity or else it would minimize the expected punishment of the tainted person. Just wait and watch.

Life is like a journey. People will join you and leave you – sometimes with your consent, sometimes without it or sometimes ditching you in between. Never loose your patience. Let everybody do his work. This is my firm conviction and I have survived despite ill health. If you cannot wipe out tears from the eyes of a victim, do not dare to victimize any body. These tears are priceless and attracts the sentiments of the 'Almighty' Do not try to be his victim, surrender yourself before him.

I personally feel that because of His blessings only this work on Andaman has taken this shape. My wife Aruna and daughter Komal never allowed me to break during the days of crisis. They suffered at my cost but without complaint and even today they were my source of inspiration in writing this book.

An idea was definitely floating in my mind to explore and admire the beauty of the Islands- to expose the evils prevalent in the society simultaneously. Deeply moved by the beauty of the Emerald Islands – I wrote a book in Hindi 'Andaman Nahi Hai Kala Pani' – a book which expresses my emotions with some factual details. All of a sudden conceived in the mind of Shri V.K.Singh IPS who inspired me to translate this book in English. The idea was in travail, a concept was struggling to get born which ultimately took the shape of this book in the shortest possible time. This idea travelled to a scholar (a friend) and he approved the idea gladly and sent it for publication. Sh. V.K. Singh, IPS, therefore, deserves all credibility for this publication although this is not a literal translation of the Hindi book. The monograph written by me is not merely a memoir. I have tried my level best to give an original picture of these islands as it was in past and present. The chapters as such archaeology speaks about the virginity of Island where not much researches have been carried so far. The journey in the offing deals with the natural curiosity of a duties in servent, who had to perform the official duty an adverse circumstances. Next chapter gives an isometric view of Portblair and its surrounding. Thereafter I have tried to give the life style of the Tribals in and around Andaman. The chapters that follows are about the historical background and importance of Andaman in freedom struggle. These researches centuries that the inhabitants settlers also actively participated in freedom struggle, which was so far unexposed in history. The concluding chapter on Tsunami tells us about the reconstructions of the Island after disaster.

For giving this shape to the book how can I ignore the contribution of Er. Kartik Mishra IIM a young boy with extraordinary calibre to excel in his profession, never hesitated to spare his time for me. Dr. Shweta Mishra- a silent spectator of the developments always extended her helping hands like my daughter and cared for my ill health, simultaneously. May God bless her for success in her endeavor for higher education and better prospects. My thanks to Shri Pradeep Kumar Pandey, Shri S.K. Dixit of ASI and Mr Rakesh Goswami for their kind cooperation.

Volumes could have been written on Andaman and truly speaking I was also in a fix as to from where should I start and where to finish. I have just restricted my quest and tried to familiarize the readers aspiring to go to these islands, by providing minimum required inputs. I am thankful to Prof.(Dr.) Panchanand Mishra for his blessings and gurus advise thus book. He wanted me to add a chapter on Cellular Jail and freedom fighters. Accordingly, I have added a chapter covering this aspect. The story of Sher Ali was popular but not so well exposed and I thought it to be appropriate to dedicate this book for this National Freedom Fighter.

Before I conclude, I express my sincere gratitude to all those writers whose name figure in the 'Appendix' for the inputs which helped me in concluding this work. I am also thankful to my Parents and my brothers always encouraged me at every door step in completing this book I owe a lot to them.

My collegues Mr Rakesh Sinha and Md. Fasiuddeen for extending their extreme cooperatin. Dr. Rashida Iqbal, Cuator National Mamorial Cellular Jail, Portblair for giving impacts about Cellular Jail, Portblair.

I acknowledge my thanks and gratitude to seniors officers Shri Ranjeet Sinha, IPS, Jawed Ahmed, IPS and Shri Shakti Sinha, IAS, Chief Secy Andaman for their valuable comments on this book.

Last but least, I am very much obliged to Shri M.L. Gupta, Rajesh Publications to be with me always for bringing out this monograph successively.

Jai Prakash Mishra
e.mail: jaiprakash.mishra@yahoo.com
Chaitra Navratra 2013

CONTENTS

1

The Journey in the Offing

All of a sudden my Cell phone became active "Hey who are you?

"I am Bhattacharya- Sir." - What happend? He was a bit serious but was trying to laugh. In these electronic devises you don't have the facility to guess " who is on the another side- his mood and sentiments. Of course, it is possible with the human beings only - the so called 'Homo Sapiens'. A wonderful creature of the nature and probably dieties remained eager for incarnation to interact with the human being from the close quarter.

"Tell me - What happened? Is everything OK?

Nothing Sir - But what are you doing?

Dining or what else? You know my routine.

OK- then I will talk later.

Tell me - Bhattacharya. Don't mind.

Tell me what happend? .... Hello - Hell .... Phone was disconnected.

I had my food. Some how I could finish but the phone call haunted all along. Why he gave me a ring? That too in the night?

Whenever you get some unusual message a negative thought develops in your mind. Perhaps something is wrong. It may not be that always but we always think in that direction. It is a matter of research - why negative thinking prevails always? Obviously, I was a bit disturbed. The only remedy left …… was to contact Bhattacharya again. He was my colleague. We worked together for several years- we shared good moments and ordeals as well. He along with mayukh was standing at my back when the doctors had clearly denied my treatment on the pretext of deteriorating condition. They fought with the doctors.

I was admitted and subsequently discharged. Why he will call? Definitely something was wrong.

The Cell Phone again became active - Sir, listen carefully – Nothing to wrong. Don't take it as a bad news. We are also very much concerned about your ill health. It is destined. We will take care of everything.

'Oh but tell me what happened? "Transfer order has been issued. You have been transferred to Port Blair?"

I was stunned. My wife was starring me.

"What happened"

"Nothing."

I left the dining table and retired to my bed room. She followed to my bed room. She followed me - and repeated" tell me - what happened? Comeon share with me."

I have been transferred to Port Blair in Andaman and Nicobar Islands. 'But why?' she failed to lelish. Have you committed any mistake?

"Mistake - what you mean to say – " It is a routine business. Transfer is not a punishment one has to face it in his service career irrespective of his choice." I had tried to pacify her?

Then, why only Andaman. They should have cared for your ill health? She was not ready to accept their development. My innocent daughter was staring at me standing on my front. She did not participate in the conversation but was able to guess that something wrong had taken place.

Suddenly my wife controlled herself. She asked my daughter to go to bed. The voice was changed "Never mind – be bold? When we have not done anything wrong, face this as a challenge.

I understand that physically and economically you may not be that strong but negative thoughts should not come in your way. My wife encouraged me. Show a brave face and take everything as a challenge. Only thing if they were suspecting something wrong the authorities should have enquired before taking action. Any action after that would have been more appreciable. She injected fresh energy in my body and I started thinking in a positive way. I did not deter when my boss advised me to call on the seniors with unconditional apology. What for? Why should I go for that? I had not committed any wrong. Of all ranks and People of all ranks and files are living there. I possibly refused his advise and started planning in a different way.

Frederic J. Mout wrote a book on Andaman long back in 1863. He has given the vivid account of the Islands Near the centre of the track of one of the greatest highways of commerce, traversed by the ships of the most civilized and enlightened nations of modern times, lie a small group of islands, the name and position of which may be found in the map, although our knowledge of them is in general very limited. Forming an almost invisible dot on the map of the world, the civilization both of the East and of the West has passed them by without in any way affecting the condition of their inhabitants. In these islands man is probably still in the same condition in which he was when they were first settled - a state not only simple and primitive, but lower even than that of the natives of these remote islands of the sea that lie far beyond the bounds of civilization. Their inhabitants acknowledge no law to restrain and guide them in life. Not only, have they no knowledge of supreme Being, but they are even destitute of such a rude system of religious faith as is generally found even amongst men in the most savage state. Their language is harsh and disagreeable, in an imperfect state of development, barely sufficient for the expression of their few and simple wants. Totally ignorant of agriculture, they have no means of making provision for the future, and must be satisfied with such fruits and herbs as the earth spontaneously produces, or with the shell-fish they pick up on the shore. Their habitations are of that primitive and simple construction which suffices for the necessities of savage tribes constantly moving from place to place.

The Andaman Archipelago, the group of islands to which we allude, is situated in the Bay of Bengal, near the meridian of 93 deg.E., and between the 10th and 15th parallels of North latitude. The largest and most important of the islands is that termed the Great Andaman, the configuration of which is remarkable in one respect, namely that, consisting of three great tracts of land, divided from each other by narrow passages, it forms apparently one great island. About twenty miles to the southward is situated a second island, which, being considerably smaller than the other, is termed the Little Andaman. The surrounding waters are studded in many directions with numerous small islets, many of them exceedingly pretty and picturesque in appearance, rising as they do like beautiful oases in the wild waste of ocean that lashes their rocky shores. All of them are clothed with the richest tropical vegetation, which from the level of the lowest swamp to the summit of the highest hill, grows in that unrestrained profusion in which Nature indulges in such climates. the entire group is surrounded in every direction by a natural fortress of coral reefs, which, extending for many miles, guards the approach to the islands, and in stormy weather, or in dark nights, renders it a matter of no little difficulty, and attended with considerable danger, to attempt to land upon them.

The inhabitants of the Andamans have always been considered one of the most savage races on the face of the earth, whom civilization has yet found it impossible to tame, or even almost to approach. From the earliest records we have, down to the most recent descriptions of their appearance and character, all accounts agree in this unfavourable representation of them With such an unevitable reputation, and the opportunities of obtaining an accurate knowledge of them having been known with regard to their actual condition, their habits and modes of life, or their origin and peculiar characteristics, the study has become difficult. The study of the race to which they belong also involves one of those ethnological problems which yet remain to be solved; and although we may not be able to settle the question, it may at any rate be in our power, by means of the personal observations we have had an opportunity of making, to furnish some data by which a solution may be rendered easier to other inquiries.

In giving a more minute description of the Great Andaman, it may be observed that its western section is about forty-four miles in length, while its breadth may be computed at about an average of fourteen miles. In this part of the island is the magnificent harbour called Port Cornwallis, which, being locked in by land, affords a secure refuge for ships. The surface of this spacious natural harbour is diversified by several small islands, in one of which, in they year 1791, a place of refuge for such mariners as had the misfortune to be shipwrecked on that dreaded coast, and a burial settlement for those who sank under their hardship, were founded. They were discovered, however, to be in several respects unsuited for the purpose intended, and in the course of a few years were ultimately abandoned. the principal reasons for taking such a step, after a good deal of trouble and expense, were the extreme unhealthiness of the locality that had been selected, and the great additional expenditure that was requisite in order to supply those temporarily settled there with the various necessaries of life.

The Saddle Mountain is situated to the southward of Port Cornwallis, at the distance of a few miles. It rises to a considerable height, and forms the highest point to be seen in the whole group, its elevation being about 2,400 feet. On a favourable day when the atmosphere is clear and cloudless, it is visible to the practised eye of the mariner at a distance of twenty leagues from the land.

The middle division, known as the Middle Andaman, is separated from the northern portion o the island by a narrow strait. It is somewhat larger than the latter, extending in length to fifty miles, and being fifteen miles in width. The narrow strait is quite innavigable, and on examining it we found that, at a distance of six miles from its eastern outlet, it became a mere mud marsh at low water. At its north-western extremity, on the other hand, it was ascertained that it opened into a fine broad expanse, forming an excellent and capacious harbour, with secure anchorage for ships, at the extremity of which is Interview Island, one of the largest detached islets of the whole group.

The South Andaman is forty-three miles in length, and its average breadth about the same as that of the Middle division. On its eastern side there are two commodious harbours, to which the names of Port Meadows and Port Blair have been given. There are also town harbours on its western coast, distinguished as Port Mouat and Port Campbell. the strait by which the Southern Andaman is separated from the Middle is navigable throughout its whole extent; and near its western extremity is an extremely fine harbour, which has only recently been discovered by Major Haughton, the second superintendent of Port Blair. On the southern side of the South Andaman, from which it is separated by Macpherson's Straits, another small island is situated. It is known by the name of Rutland Island, and is nearly ten miles long, by four broad. The northern extremity of this island rises to a considerable height.

In the course of our voyage we sighted the Little Andaman, but after due consideration did not deem it advisable to land and examine it. In the first place, we knew that it contained no good harbours at which we could conveniently land, in order to carry on any explorations in the interior; and what weighed most with us, we were aware that it possessed none of those requisites of which we were specially in search, and was in no way adapted for a settlement to which convicts might be safely conveyed, and where they might be profitably employed.

This was the only limited knowledge I was heard about these pretty islands. I had been to Port Blair in the year 2004 as a tourist and had a stay of four days. The tour operator was much commercial in his attitude and he took us only to those places which were profitable for him. Commercially, my queste for knowledge about the Island remained unfulfilled. I became satisfied when I went through the Gazetteer written by Kiran Dhingra which was published by Oxford in 2005. The information incorporated in this book are more authentic.

Situated between the 92nd and 94th meridians of East latitude and 6th and 14th parallels of North latitude, the Andaman and Nicobar Islands from part of a long, irregular chain that seems to continue the Eastern Himalayan ranges through Mynmar's Arakan Yoma southwards in an arch over 1100 km of sea into Sumatra. The wide curve of these Islands encloses the Andaman Sea and separates it from the Bay of Bengal, albeit imperfectly, with many channels for the waters to mingle. In the north, dividing it from the mainland of south Asia and Myanmar at Cape Negrais, is the Preparis North Channel, which stretches or a width of 103 km till Preparis Island, the first of the islands that comprise this chain; in the south, the Great Channel, stretching 144 km, while providing safe passage for ships on the main sea route to Singapore, keeps the tip of the Greater Nicobar Island from joining up with the northern point of Sumatra. In between there are numerous straits that separate the 204 islands – 572, if all the islets and rocks be faithfully counted. The biggest of these straits is the Ten Degree channel (so called because the 10th North parallel passes through it), 139 km wide and 1399m deep, that, lying between Little

Andaman group to its north and Car Nicobar to its south, divides the chain into the Andaman group of islands and the Nicobar group. The great depth of these channels - like long fissuries in the ocean bed - and of the waters to the east and west of the chain, lends credence to the hypothesis that the Andaman and Nicobar Islands were never part of the South East Asian mainland, nor a complete strip of land at some time, but the summits of two distinct submarine ranges.

Land area of 8249 sq km, form part of India as the Union Territory of the Andaman and Nicobar Islands. They are the outermost posts of the country, with a sea-route distance o 1397 km between Port Blair, the headquarters of the Union Territory, and Calcutta.

South of Little Andaman and the Ten degree Channel lie the Nicobar Islands in a chain 278 km long. The 1841 sq. km of land that this group covers is divided over some twenty-two islands, ten of them uninhabited, and perhaps the only remaining example of virgin equatorial jungle in the world. Car Nicobar Island lies at the northern limit of this group. Of the twelve inhabited islands in the Nicobars, it has the highest density of population. Its flat, round shape has been compared to Australia but there the comparison must end, for Car Nicobar is only 127 sq. km in area, and its perimeter can be covered in forty minutes at moderate vehicular pace. To the south of Car Nicobar, at a distance of about 35 km, lies the small and inaccessible island of Batti Malv. Southwards by 45 km gets us to Chaura, the third of the predominantly coral islands of the group. Chaura is, like the other two islands, small being only 7.25 sq. km in area; flat except for a cylindrical outcrop of rock in the south east, that looks with its contiguous lower portion.

These, as one moves southwards by approximately 13 km, are Teresa and Bompoka, huddling close together across a turbulent channel 2.8 km wide; Kamorta, Trinkat, Katchall, and Nancowry arranged to form the Nancowry harbour, one of the safest known and certainly the best in the Nicobars; and, at a little distance North to Kamorta and east to Chaura, the uninhabited Tillangchong and the tiny Isle of Man.

The southern Nicobars, on the other hand, have dense vegetation and high forest trees, and are a prime example of tropical jungle. Lying across the sombrero Channel from the nancowry group, are, principally, Kondul, Little Nicobar, and Great Nicobar, the last ebing the largest, at 86 sq. km, of the Nicobar group of islands, and the end of the chain. Of the several smaller islands, like outlaying satellites, that complete this group, mention may be made of Meroe, Treis, Trak, Pulo Milo, Menchal, and Megapod, the last now a wildlie sanctuary for the Megapode, an endemic species of bird found at one time in abundance here.

Early geological studies were carried out by Dr. P.H. Rink of the Galatea (1847), F. Von Hochstetter of the Novara (1866), and Dr. R.D. Oldham (1885). In later years, G.H. Tipper (1911), E.R. Gee (1926), and scientists of the Geological Survey of India, among them M.S. Srinivasan, M.S. Krishnan, K.K. Ray, S.S. Saha, S. Bandopadhyay, and H. Nandi, carried on the work. Earlier it was supposed that asbestos, chromite, coal, building stone, and even marble might be found on the Islands. Later surveys found limestone and clay for making bricks, but very little mineral of quantity or value to make mining a commercially viable proposition. The 1970s thus witnessed oil explorations on these Islands. Oil was indeed located, but at such depths under the sea bed that it belied hopes of commercial exploitation and quickly dispelled the expectations of striking it rich as in neighbouring Indonesia.

This narrow, irregular chain of islands is everywhere hilly and covered by a dense mantle of lush green tropical vegetation that has survived the rapid growth of population. Sandy beaches and encircled by the clear white of foam from the breakers, is a singularly refreshing sight that never fails to charm. It is more striking seen from the air, when the colours of the surrounding waters, from shades of opaque turquoise to clear sapphire and lapis lazuli, provide a perfect contrast to the emeralds green of the land. The aerial view also affords a clear picture of the hilly featues and undulations of the land.

For a place so close to the equator, temperatures in the Andaman and Nicobar Islands are moderate. Even more markedly, the diference between maximum and minimum temperatures, which is as much as 30 degree -10 degree C in most parts of the islands get rain eight months of the year, from the south West monsoon from May till September and the North East from November till January. The south West normally arrives on 20 May, accompanied by high winds and gales and the possibility of cyclones. From June to August, there is persistent and heavy rain, winds up to 20 knots, low visibility, sudden squalls and the virtual cessation of all fishing activity.

A reliable history of the Andaman Islands may be dated from 1789, when Lieutenant Archibald Blair came to the archipelago to execute a brief of the Governor General of India, Lord Cornwallis, to survey the land, raise the British flag, and set up a harbour where ships could refit themselves in times of war or distress. Before that, the accounts available may at best be categorized as travelogues, some of them the products of vivid imagination strong on colour, and interesting to read, but of little value to the serious historian. Till the occupation of the islands and actual encounters with their inhabitants proved otherwise, it was the popular notion that the inhabitants were saset of fierce cannibals with dog faces and tails, who preferred human flesh to fish or fowl, and who spared no shipwrecked sailor from a loathsome fate. No one who wrote about the islands in the early days seemed to have ventured on land to bravely gather empirical evidence.

The earliest reference appears at about the start of the Christian Era. In the writings of the famous astronomer, mathematician, and geographer, Claudius Ptolemaeus, better known as Ptolemy, there is mention of a group of islands occupied by cannibals that the called Agadaemon. That group of islands has been taken to be the andamans, and the name a rendition of Agedaman, or Angdeman, or Andaman. Some chronicles would also have it that there is an even earlier reference, in the Ramayana, to the islands as the first choice of a site for a bridge to Lanka to rescue Sita. This led to association of the islands with Hanuuman, and to the malayns calling the inhabitants Handuman, and thence Andaman. In the seventh century AD, the Chinese traveler I – Tsing, who appears to have been to both the Andamn and the Nicobar Islands which he calls the Andaman and Yeng-t'o-mang or the 'Land of the Naked' respectively – gives one of the most credible descriptions of the place when he describes the transactions with the tribals involving the barter of coconuts for iron.

Despatched to the Andaman Islands to assess their potential for the setting up of a port that could provide facilities to mercantile vessels in passage through the Bay of Bengal, and fortified refugee to the British navy in times of war, Lieutenant Blair set sail for the Andamans from Calcutta on 20 December and reached the Andaman waters on 29 December 1788. In the three months he was there, he surveyed the west coast of Great Andaman, moving southwards from Inter Island to Port Campbell, and round Mac Pherson's Strait to the east coast. Blair's report, with a precise hydrographic description of the coastline, a judicious assessment of the harbours, and a remarkably faithful account of the geophysical features of the island, carried a recommendation that the capacious harbour to the southeast of South Andaman would be the best site to locate a settlement; and so impressed were his superiors at Calcutta that within a space of three months, by September 1789, on a report dispatched on 9 June 1789, he found himself back in the Andamans, with the commission that he himself undertake the task of setting up the colony in the harbour of his choosing, and christen it Port Cornwallis. With him, on this expedition, were Lieutenant Colebrooke and Lieutenant Wales, and a detachment of about 200 mechanics, craftsmen, sepoys, and labourers.

Choosing as his site Chatham Island, a small island about 12 acres in area, set well within the harbour, connected to the main island by a causeway at low tide, and easy to defend against hostile tribals, Blair bagan be clearing the irest, planting grass on the hill tops and vegetables and fruits on the lower slopes, and erecting shelters for them, storehouses for the equipment, and a hospital. The work was undertaken with such managerial skill- supplies and replenishments coming in from Penang and Calcutta, visits to the mainland being organized for the settlers, and the autochthons being fended off with gifts, gestures of friendship and the minimum of force - that within a year, Blair was able to move to constructing a wharf, laying a road from Phoenix Bay to Navy Bay, planning agriculture on the island's westerly side, an considering the possibilities of the timber trade. By 1791, the settlers were bringing in their families, and it seemed that the Andamanese had reconciled to their presence. At any rate, Blair seemed to have through so, and wrote to Calcutta in 1792 to that effect.

From the day it shifted, the new settlement ran into the sort of misfortune that would have touched a familiar chord with the danes, of the four ships that moved out of Calcutta, laden with provisions and 360 settlers, the Juno, with ninety settlers on board, coming to grief in an unexpected cyclone, did not reach. Undeterred, the remained got down to work. The plan adopted in the first settlement was repeated faithfully, even to the choosing of a site on an island connected to the mainland by an isthmus, and to the naming of its as Chatham Island and of the harbour as Port Cornwallis. The earlier Port Cornwallis, whorn of its name, became the Old Harbour, and remained so unglorified till, in its next occupation, it was dignified, most fittingly, with the name Port Blair.

The monsoon of 1795 brought sickness and misery afresh taking fifty lives. The death of the surgeon in January 1796 proved the last straw. Every settler had by then had enough and wanted to leave the place. The council of Directors finally took the decision to close down the settlement, and on 8 February 1796, issued instructions to withdraw from the Islands. The 270 convicts and 550 free men, women, and children then there were shifted back, the convicts to Penang and the rest to Calcutta, and the settlement as well as the attempt at colonization was abandoned in May 1796.

The Andamanese went back to their isolation, and for the next sixty years remained undisturbed and unapproached.

As per the 1991 census, 39 islands of this territory were found to be inhabited. These islands include Ross Island which is completely under the occupation of the Defence Authorities and Chatham Islands which is connected by a bridge with Port Blair but is not treated as a part of Port Blair. Out of the 38 islands, 25 islands are located in Andaman district and 13 in the Nicobar district. Except Nicobarese and primitive tribal, the rest are the people from the mainland refugees from former East Pakistan (now Bangladesh), repatriates from Sri Lanka and Burma, resettled Ex-Servicemen and descendents of the prisoners held at Port Blair. There is another set of population (migrants) from Tamil Nadu, Andhra Pradesh, Kerala and Bihar (particularly from Ranchi) who are labourers. The population of these islands is a heterogeneous one, with a mixture of diverse communities from the mainland. So Andaman & Nicobar Island is a miniature India. People of all the stages in India live in these Islands in harmony with their own culture.

As already mentioned, in Andaman & Nicobar Islands people from different regions, religions, races, faiths etc. continue to live together in a peaceful manner. Some were invited to these islands and some came to these islands on employment and some started economic actives relating to trade, commerce and industry. So the population of these islands can be broadly divided into four groups. They are 1) Tribals, 2) Andaman Indians, 3) New Settlers and 4) Govt. employees form the mainland.

The aboriginals or the tribals of these islands are the original inhabitants. The total number of the tribal population as per 1991 census was 26770 which is 9.5% of the total population of Andaman & Nicobar islands.

It has always been my endeavour to know about the things, to assess a situation, to read available materials before arriving at a conclusion or taking a decision regarding anything whatsoever. This peculiar state of mind always presented me to enter into any controversy as to compromise with my self respect. Other day when one of my seniors passed a sarcastic remark "Then you prefer to go to 'Kalapani?"

"Sorry Sir, I beg to differ. I do not know what do you know about Kalapani. These words are used in India only and I do not know why people prefer to use this word. I anyhow, took leave and returned back. Both words 'kala' and 'pani' are hindi words and do not find mention in the English dictionary. The literal meaning is 'Black Water.' I have never seen black water anywhere. History tells is that these words were borrowed by the Britishers to terrorise the participants of Indian freedom struggle. It became a synonymous of torture in the year to come. What 'kala pani'? People are living there. People are visiting there as tourist. People are serving their as public servants. Senior police officer, bureaucrats and the Governor are camping there as representative of Govt. of India. They are not enjoying any punishment. Central command of the Army is keeping vigil even round the clock in the interest of the nation. Among them, where do I stay. I am a part of administration. For me there cannot be separate rule. Although I was aware of the ill intention behind my transfer, but it could not deter me. I became more bold and planned to land at Port Blair as early as possible. I was availing the transit leave and about the join the Island in the mid of September, 2007.

A few days before leaving, I called on one of my friends who had a good Archeological background. He had worked in Andaman for years and collected a lot of inputs of the islands. Before giving a final shape to the journey, I was planning to be more familiar with the background of the Islands before facing and observing the people from the close quarter.

Dr. Mishra I want to trouble you?

Dr. Mishra was taking a sun bath in his residential lawn wearing a Kurta and pyajama with a new paper in his hand. He pushed his spects at the right place which were coming down. He was not expecting me rather. He stood up and the moment he saw me smiled, offered a chair "you are most welcome. Be comfortable. Tell me what can I do for you."

Nothing as you might be knowing — Yes — Yes— he interrupted – I have heard you are going to Andaman?

You are fortunate. You are going to a beautiful place.

Andaman Island sites containing glass are most numerous around Port Blair and the places where the so-called homes of the Andamanese were established. For example, Lapicque noted bases of glass bottles among other objects in an abandoned encampment in South Andaman. Although the "homes" no longer stand, the beaches of Ross Island, which overlooks Port Blair and was once the headquarters of the British penal settlement, are strewn with colourful pieces of glass rubbed smooth by abrasion. Most of these have resulted from natural breakage, although some may have ended up on shell middens, not only for cutting purposes, but also perhaps for their aesthetic value. In view of this, it was necessary to exercise caution in reporting such material, especially since some middens around Port Blair were contributed by Burmese convicts. Therefore, the sites described here have been selected because of their distance from Port Blair, and only those that have been carefully examined and sampled by Cooper are discussed here. Cipriani's excavation of the midden near Beehive Hill, on Middle Andaman Island, had yielded five human burials, besides pottery and flakes of what he mistook as obsidian. In 1986, Cooper conducted a careful search of the surface of the midden as well as of the exposed sections, but she did not find any obsidian splinters, though pieces of glass and stone flakes were fairly abundant Furthermore, it may be noted that there is no source of obsidian in the Andamans. Among the glass artifacts collected from the midden at Beehive Hill, there are eight flakes and twenty chips. Seven of the flakes are of green glass and one is of white. A few of them are partially flaked. The chips are all of green glass.

Two glass pieces that bear evidence of working were recovered by Cooper from the surface of a site near Lakhimpur in North Andaman Island and from a midden on Swamp Island in Austen Strait The piece from Lakhimpur has a convex surface that has been flaked partly to form a sharp edge. The glass flake from Swamp Island is roughly diamond-shaped and is flaked along the edges on the dorsal surface. The ventral side, along the straight edge, is also flaked.

Long back, I heard a dictum – life a mistery to be lived and not a problem to be solved. I always remember these lines and I feel a short of satisfaction. It prevents me from getting frustrated and sometimes sparks me to think or to do a fresh or even something better. Arm with the knowledge of the Islands I kept on waiting for my departure from the mainland to the capital city of Port Blair – down south in the Bay of Bengal and looking like dancing damcels in the bay. A group of more than 530 Islands floating together gives a vivid picture of nature. The aerial view is just to be observed and no word can narrate the beauty of the islands from the sky. The time had come, and I left for Kolkata for a direct flight to Port Blair. It is the only city in the ground of Islands which is having an airodrome. Direct flights are there from Kolkata and Chennai whereas hoping flights are there from the national capital of Delhi. Besides the Indian

Airlines, the national carrier, private aircrafts are also operating from Delhi, Kolkata as well as from Chennai. The flights start from 5.20 AM and all the flights returned back from Port Blair in the forenoon. The journey takes about 2.05 hrs. from Kolkata and Chennai. Port Blair is also connected by ship from Chennai, Kolkata and Vishakhapatnam. It takes around 3 to 4 days by ship. All the ships are air conditioned and provide all facilities to the passengers in transit. Whereas the flights operate daily. The Shipping Corporation of India announces its schedule and normally the ships are available three or four times a month. The entire islands enjoy a moderate temperature and it ranges between 20 to 30 degree C. April to September is the Rainy Season and sea is normally rough during this season. Sea voyage are not advisable during this period.

It was sometime in mid of November, I boarded the Indian Airlines flights scheduled for Port Blair. All the mysteries was over with the announcement of the Air Hostess "your attention please, you will be landing at Port Blair within a short while —!

The aircraft was in the air. I started refereshing my memory about the islands. The Andaman and Nicobar Islands were shrouded in mystery for centuries because of their inaccessibility. These are the paragon of beauty and present a landscape full with scenic and picturesque extravaganza. These islands shimmer like emeralds in the Bay of Bengal. The dense forest which cover these islands and the innumerable exotic flowers and birds create a highly poetic and romantic atmosphere. "Here the white beaches on the edge of a meandering coastline have palm trees that sway to the rhythm of the Sea. The beat of tribal drums haunt the stillness and technicolour fish steer their way through crystal clear water." This addition of strangeness to beauty which is responsible for creating the infinite romantic impact may be described in the following famous lines of Keats.

"Charmed magic casement opening on the foam of perilous seas in fair lands forlorn." The scenic beauty of Andaman &

Nicobar Islands, would create a sense of dissatisfaction and the human mind would rebel against "the whole mass of the motley facts of life". He would be guided by an irresistible desire to this paradise on earth, with invincible faith on the philosophy of Wordsworth: "Our cheerful faith, that all which we behold is full of blessing".

The unparalleled beauty of these islands, create in men a love of nature with a caressing tenderness, a wistful fondness for all its delicate nuances. The enveloping atmosphere with its subtle harmonies of light and shade, fragrance and exhales the paradise, visionary splendours, and the music of the birds that defies definition would develop creative and constructive feelings in the hearts of those people who come here to enjoy the beauty of nature. He would like to rebel against the stereotyped moulds and forms into which life is so called 'modernman' is cast. He would be under the impact of the complex mood of infinite longing and tragic helplessness, "the yearning that craves for expression, yet defies expression, the inconclusive struggle between emotional apprehension of life and the articulation that must transcend personal emotion".

The Andaman and Nicobar Islands have great maritime importance. During the British period political leaders considered dangerous to the interests of the Raj and other dreaded criminals were deported from mainland to the Cellular Jail- the Indian Bastille, situated on the sea coast of Atlanta Point in the North-Eastern part of Port Blair. Thus these islands were infamously known as the 'Black Water Prison' or 'Kala Pani'.

The Andaman & Nicobar are a group of picturesque Islands, big and small, inhabited and uninhabited, a total of 572 islands, islets and rocks lying in the South Eastern Part of the Bay of Bengal.They lie along an arc in long and narrow broken chain, approximately North-South over a distance nearly 800 kms. It is logical to presume a former land connection form Cape Negris at South part of Burma to Achin Head (Cape Pedro) in Andalas

(Sumatra). The flora and fauna of these islands, however, indicate that this land connection if it existed, should have been prior to the development of their present life form.

I had fastened my seat belt and started curiously waiting for the landing. The climate appeared to be very pleasant and what I saw from the sky was simply unforgettable. A group of islands with greenery were floating in the emerald sea. We came nearer and nearer and ultimately the Airhostess announced again well come to Vir Sawarkar Air Port — ! I was out of the air-port: I had posted my programme earlier but I was not aware of the set up of my office. I even did not know where to go. Where will be my place of stay? Who will look after me? What kind of food I would get? The location of my office, the nature of work in the Island – administrative and logistic support - there was a lot of thing to study before starting a fresh. There is the differences between a planned and unplanned journey. When you are sent to a place which the impression of punishment, you loose motivation. These things are not visualized by the bosses. They send you to a particular place with the stigma of punishment and expect some thing which can not be done. This place of punishment becomes a merry make up place for them and their dependants. Shamelessly they will place only for arranging all facilities for them then dependents and sometimes for friends and neighbours also. You are supposed to attend it at the cost of your self respect and reputation. Even an inkling of deviation is not tolerable. You will have to be on the burnt. How can a place be a source of enjoyment for a group of person and punishment for other? It is a matter of introspection. You will get the reply. I had come with a positive thinking of hitting all parts of the Islands before my asylum was over. I use the word 'Asylum' for this type of postings because for a middle class family, it is very difficult to sustain this type of situation. Especially, at a stage when your children are grown up and you are not in a position to shift your family at a place of posting for any reason whatsoever.

You can not visit them on well whenever you like. A single journey from Kolkata / Chennai to Port Blair will cost around 10,000/- Rs. from one side per person. It is a luxury for a public servant.

I was standing out side the exit gate holding the trolley. A policeman came and asked "Are you searching for somebody?"

From the body language, he could understand that I belonged to the same department. He disappeared and came along with a person.

"Sir – I am Swamy?" 'Pl.come.' He took my luggage and requested to follow him.

This was for the first time, I met Swamy. From him appearance, he appeared to be a gangster: something like we see in a south Indian movie. Lean and thin body, tall figure peculiar moustache, and red 'tikka' on his forehead. He directed me to be comfortable on the front seat of the old jeep which was some how in the working condition. When I tried to hit him with a satire- Swamy stared me – but kept mum. Later on I came to know that he was very fond of this jeep and was maintaining it by managing its parts which were simply out of market. Any cross comments about this vehicle was not tolerable to him. One, during my posting somebody came to me with a complaint that Swamy is seen with this office vehicle always. Was he doing it for personal use? 'No'

Then it is none of your business to go in details.

2

In Andaman

Swamy dropped me to HADDO circuit house which is around 3-4 KM from the Vir Savarkar Airport. I could feel that I was in the neat and clean city full of scenaries and hilly tracks. A room was booked in my name, in the circuit house. Swamy took the leave with request that on the next day SS Grewal would be coming to receive me. Thereafter he would take me to the office.

That was my first day at of Andaman. I was a stranger and did not know any body there. I went to the kitchen and enquired about the type of food being prepared by them. I was relaxed to know that the quality of food prepared in the guest houses at Andaman was similar to North Indian recipies.

I was aware that after five working days, I had to find out work for myself. Before Swamy could leave me alone, I put a straight question. "Please let me know Swamy the places I could visit in the weekends". Swamy was a native of Andaman as he told me. His father had come to this place in search of a job. From his body language, I could guess that he became happy with this question. He asked with the smile on his face – "Sir, if you are really interested Grewal will help you in this matter. I just give you a broad idea about the places of tourists interests in North Andaman. As he told Andaman and Nicobar islands were popularly known as the Emerald Isles. The erstwhile 'Kaala

Paani' or the Cellular Jail, now a museum was the most popular tourist spot. Other places of tourist interest include National Memorial, Marine Museum, Naval Marine Museum, Smrithika Museum, Haddo Zoological Garden, Corbyn's Cove, and other beaches, and Humphrey Gunj Memorial. Andaman Water Sports Complex at Port Blair. Chatam Saw Mill (largest in Asia), Chidiya Tapu, Marine Museum, the island of red Skibn, and Havelock were the other attractions. Corbyn's Cove, Wandoor beach, Sippighat water sports complex, Cinque island, and Jolly Buoy island were some adventurous spots on the island.

PLACE TO VISIT

Wandoor - The beautiful Wandoor beach is situated at Mahatma Gandhi marine national park, around 30 Kms from Port Blair. Nearly 15 islands are located surrounding this stretch of pristine coastline.

Mahatma Gandhi Marine National Park - Covering a huge area of 281.5 kilometer square, this national park is created out of 15 islands. It is only 29 kilometers from the major city Port Blair.

Carbyn's Cove Tourism Complex - The water near the Corbyn's Cove Tourism Complex at Andaman and Nicobar Islands has a very strong current due to which large waves rise in it. The whole view is scintillating. People visit here to see the strong waves.

Havelock Island - It is one of the few islands that is inhabited, although most of it is a natural paradise, replete with white sand beaches, coral reefs with a colourful array of aquatic life, palm trees, as well as dense forests in the interiors.

Scuba diving - There is no adventure than diving. Whether you are novice, or whether you were been diving for so many years, there is always something new, fascinating or challenging about venturing into the underwater world.

Snorkeling - Snorkeling is an adventure activity which is very popular off the Andaman Islands. If untrained, you can still indulge yourself by remaining just beneath the surface of the water and, with a little practice, you can dive up to 8 to 10 ft under water.

Trekking - One can go trekking through the nature trail from Mt. Harriet to Kalapathar and enjoy the rare forest life, flora and fauna. There are other trekking routes also at places like Chidiya Tapu."

I had a nice stay of two years in these islands. I never missed the opportunity of visiting the local library and searching the books on Andaman which were going to be bigger assets for me in the time to come. I diariesed the entire details which could have been accessible to me.

FLORA & FAUNA

These Islands are blessed with a unique' luxuriant evergreen tropical rainforest canopy, sheltering a mixed germ plasm bank, comprising of Indian, Myanmarese, Malaysian and endemic floral strain. So far, about 2200, varieties of plants have been recorded out of which 200 are endemic and 1300 do not occur in mainland India.

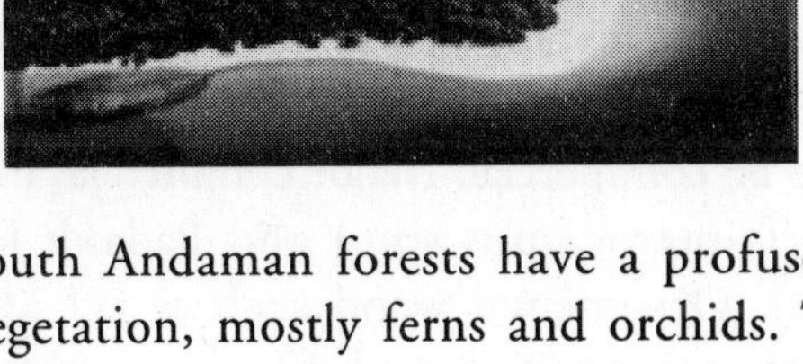

"The South Andaman forests have a profuse growth of epiphytic vegetation, mostly ferns and orchids. The Middle Andamans harbours mostly moist deciduous forests. North

Andamans is characterised by the wet evergreen type, with plenty of woody climbers. The north Nicobar Islands (including Car Nicobar and Battimalv) are marked by the complete absence of evergreen forests, while such forests form the dominant vegetation in the central and southern islands of the Nicobar group. Grasslands occur only in the Nicobars, and while deciduous forests are common in the Andamans, they are almost absent in the Nicobars". This a typical forest coverage is made-up of twelve types namely (1) Giant evergreen forest (2) Andamans tropical evergreen forest (3) Southern hilltop tropical evergreen forest (4) Cane brakes (5) Wet bamboo brakes (6) Andamans semi-evergreen forest (7) Andamans moist deciduous forest (8) Andamans secondary moist deciduous forest (9) Littoral forest (10) Mangrove forest (11) Brackish water mixed forest (12) Submontane hill valley swamp forest. The present forest coverage is claimed to be 86.2% of the total land area.

TIMBER

Andaman Forest is abound in plethora of timber species numbering 200 or more, out of which about 30 varieties are considered to be commercial. Major commercial timber species are Gurjan (Dipterocarpus spp.) and Padauk (Pterocarpus dalbergioides). Ornamental wood such as (1) Marble Wood (Diospyros marmorata) (2) Padauk (Pterocarpus dalbergioides), (3) Silver Grey (a special formation of wood in white chuglam)

(4) Chooi (Sageraea elliptical and (5) Kokko (Albizzia lebbeck) are noted for their pronounced grain formation. Padauk being steadier than teak is widely used for furniture making. Burr and the Buttress formation in Andaman Padauk are World famous for their exceptionally unique charm and figuring. Largest piece of Buttress known from Andaman was a dining table of 13'x 7'. The largest piece of Burr was again a dining table to seat eight persons at a time. The holy Rudraksha (Elaeocarps sphaericus) and aromatic Dhoop/Resin trees also occur here.

FAUNA

This tropical rain forest despite its isolation from adjacent land masses is surprisingly enriched with many animals.

MAMMALS - About 50 varieties of forest mammals are found to occur in Andaman & Nicobar Islands, most of them are understood to be brought in from outside and are now considered endemic due to their prolonged insular adaptation. Rat is the largest group having 26 species followed by 14 species of bat. Among the larger mammals there are two endemic varieties of wild pig namely Sus Scrofa andamanensis from Andaman and S.S.nicobaricus from Nicobar. The spotted deer Axis axis, Barking deer and Sambar are found in Andaman District. Interview island in Middle Andaman holds a fairly good stock of feral elephants.

These elephants were brought in for forest work by a private contractor who subsequently left them loose.

Butterflies and Moths - With about 225 species, the Andaman & Nicobar Islands house some of the larger and most spectacular butterflies of the world. Ten species are endemic to these Islands. Mount Harriet National Park is one of the richest areas of butterfly and moth diversity on these Islands.

Shells - Shells are perhaps the most colourful and fascinating objects known to man other than Gems since time immemorial. They served as money, ornaments, musical instruments, drinking cups, in magic and in the making of fine porcelains. They were also the symbols in rituals and religious observances, and the returning pilgrims wore them as a token of divine pardon.

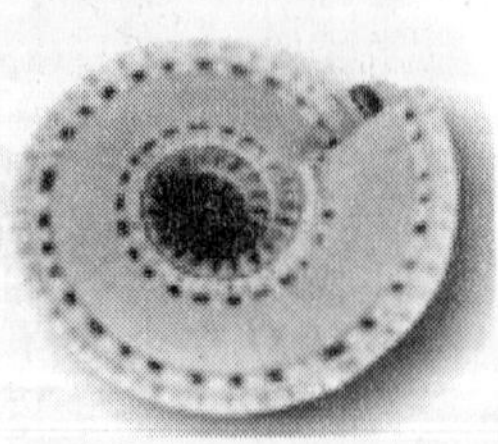

These islands are traditionally known for their shell wealth specially Turbo,Trochus, Murex and Nautilus. Earliest recorded commercial exploitation began during 1929. Shells are important to these islands because some like Turbo, Trochus & Nautilus etc. are being used as novelties supporting many cottage industries producing a wide range of decorative items & ornaments. Shells such as Giant clam, Green mussel and Oyster support edible shellfishery, a few like Scallop, Clam and Cockle are burnt in kiln to produce edible lime.

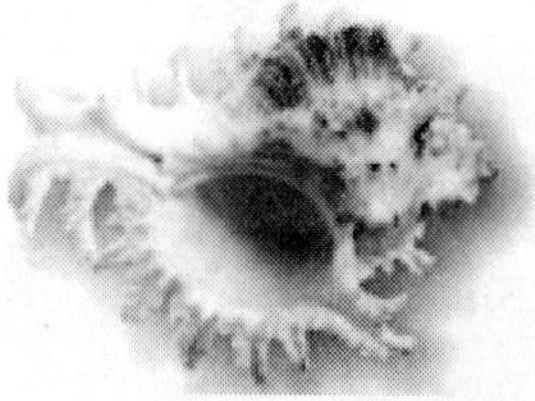

The Univalve or one shell group belongs to the class Gastropoda having more than 80,000 species. Sacred Chank belongs to this group. Their body, in the course of development, go through a complicated process, 'torsion' i.e. the visceral mass is twisted though 90 degree together with the shell that covers it. Under mysterious circumstances many a time this process proceeds in the reverse direction thus creating an abnormal shell which otherwise lives like a normal shell. A classic example is the most wanted left-handed chank.

The Bivalve or Pelecypoda has about 20,000 living species. Majority of then burrows in sand or mud such as Pearl Oyster, Wing oyster, Giant clam etc. A third group, which is comparatively smaller, is called Cephalopoda, which includes Octopus, Squid, Nautilus etc. The soft body animal, which lives inside the shell, is covered with a thick layer of specialised epithelium cells known as rnantle, which in turn secretes a two tier shell material making the shell. The outer layer having a different colour pattern is organic in constitution, technically called 'periostracum'. Calcium ions from the environment are absorbed into the blood and deposited evenly under this layer. The next inner layer is called 'nacre' or 'mother of pearl' responsible for the pearly lustre common to many shells.

CORALS

Corals belong to a large group of animals known as Coelenterata (stinging animals) or Cnidaria (thread animals). Corals grow slow, they have type wise site specific growth rates. The massive forms may grow upto 2 cm. in diameter and upto 1 cm in height a year, whereas, delicate branching forms grow between 5 to 10 cm. per annum. A true reef building stony coral may be unisexual or bisexual. They breed together once in a year at a pre-determined time after dusk. This process, at places is so intense that the water stays pinkish till next morning.

A large number of baby corals are released in the open ocean this way. After sometime these baby corals settle over a suitable substratum and start forming new colonies through asexual reproduction. Their morphological features change with the environment in which they settle. Due to this peculiar character they are often called 'Plastic animals.'

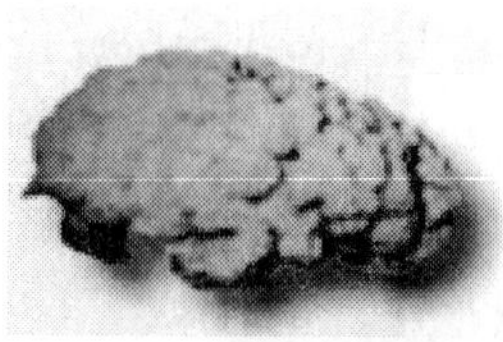

Stony corals could be broadly divided into reef builders and non-reef builders, the reef builders are called hermatypic whereas others are known as ahermatypic corals. The reef builders possess hard calcareous skeleton and need sunlight like plants to survive. On the other hand, the non-reef builders are devoid of a true stony framework and can live well without sunlight. A few among them are capable of making protein based solidified skeleton.

FISHES

Each life form in the sea is confined to its own particular zone, where pressure, light, temperature and salinity are more or less constant. In this stable environment some creatures have

remained unchanged throughout their entire history. The now famous Coelacanth, one of the groups of fishes thought to have been extinct for 60 million years, has remained essentially like its relatives as they appear in fossils. Fishes are the masters of water world. For more than 360 million years they have inhabited it. Today we have about 40,000 varieties of fishes known to science.

They range in size from 10 mm (Philippine Gobie) to 21m. (whale shark). Some are flattened, others inflated, many spindle shaped, a few snakelike, still others are compressed depending on the environment in which they live or particular way of life.

MARINE AQUARIUM

Marine fish and animal keeping still has a certain mystique attached to it. This is one of the most complicated aspects of live stock management. The animal husbandry involved in it is mainly nurtured through water chemistry and microbiology. The tropical coral reef inhabitants are generally maintained in glass boxes known to us as marine aquariums. These animals turn 'fragile' under captive atmosphere because the natural system to which they belong is so heterogeneous, complex and dynamic with every tide bringing in a different condition that is so difficult to create artificially. However, since May 1853 when the first tropical marine aquarium was made public in London, much has been understood and we are now able to practice a system where these animals are acclimatized and taught to be happy in their new environs.

STATE BIRD

Andaman Wood Pigeon is an endemic bird, which is found only in Andaman and Nicobar group of islands. This bird is of the size of a domestic pigeon with longer tail. This bird has whitish head with checkerboard pattern on neck. The upper parts are dark slate grey in colour and underparts are pale blue grey Metallic green sheen on upper side and reddish bill with yellowish tip and purplish red orbital skin are identification characters. The bird lives in dense broadleaved evergreen forest.

Dugong-State Andaman

Andaman Wood Pigeon is an endemic bird, which is found only in Andaman and Nicobar group of islands. This bird is of the size of a domestic pigeon with longer tail. This bird has whitish head with checkerboard pattern on neck. The upper parts are dark slate grey in colour and underparts are pale blue grey Metallic green sheen on upper side and reddish bill with yellowish tip and purplish red orbital skin are identification characters. The bird lives in dense broadleaved evergreen forest.

Dugong - State Andaman

Dugong, an endangered marine mammal, also known as Sea Cow, is only strictly marine mammal, which is herbivorous. It mainly feeds on sea-grass and other aquatic vegetation. Dugong is distributed in shallow tropical waters in Indo-Pacific Region. The animal is about three-metre length and weighs about 400 kg. In India Dugong is reported from Gulf of Kutch, Gulf of Mannar, Palk Bay and Andaman & Nicobar Islands. Within Andaman & Nicobar Islands Dugong has been reported from Ritchie"s Archipelago, North Reef, Little Andaman and parts of Nicobars.

Andaman Padauk - State Tree

Andaman Padauk is a tall deciduous tree found only in Andaman. It grows upto height of 120 feet. The timber is highly prized for making furniture. Burr and Buttress formation add charm to the tree and used in making unique furniture.

Water Resources

In any region, surface water resources (rivers, lakes) form the major sources of water for drinking, agricultural and industrial uses as well as for household needs. Since the individual islands of this territory are small in area, there is no possibility of presence of major rivers. So, only a few streams of a few kilometers in length are seen in the Islands. The streams are locally called as "Nallahs", meaning streams or small rivers. Andaman & Nicobar Islands receive, on an average, an annual rainfall of a little more than 30mm. the precipitation received from both the south west and north east monsoon is spread over a period of six to eight months. Besides the rainfall, the other sources of water are the surface water and ground water which are the direct result of the rainfall received by the area itself. In the Andaman district, the important streams are (a) Kalpong Nallah (river) in North Andaman, (b) Vasundhra Nallah, (c) Wrightmyo Nallah, (d) Dhania Nallah and (E) Sona Nallah in South Andaman, (f) Rangat Nallah, (g) Badam Nallah, (h) Thoratang Nallah, (i) Picture Nallah, (j) CFO nallah, (k) Korang Nallah and (1) Panchavadi Nallah in Middle Andaman. In the Nicobar District, the streams are visible only in Great Nicobar Island. The important streams are (a) Galathia river, (b) Alexandria river, (c) Dongmar river (small). In Car Nicobar there is no nallah. There is no lake or tank in these Islands, except the Thilthamman tank which is situated in the heart of these streams (nallahs) are that they are short in length and swift in flow towards east or west, resulting in a quick run off into the sea. During the rain season, the (nallahs) steams are full of water and scarcity of water occurs only for four months. Even in the rainy season, scarcity of water for industrial activies in there in almost all the Islands since there is no dam in these Islands except one name Dhanikhari dam in Port Blair.

As far as Port Blair, the only urban centre in the islands having a population of around 50,000is concerned the drinking water is being supplied from Dhanikar dam which was constructed in, and has been supplying potable water since and end of 1973. This dam's storage capacity is 900 million gallons and is capable of supplying 1.5 million gallons of water pwe day to the Port Blair city. Thiltamman tank, near God Vetrimalai Murugan Temple, was supplying drinking water to Port Balir city. But after the construction of the Dhanikari dam the tank is not utilized as a source of drinking water. It also reserves a considerable amount of water throughout the year, and there is no other major storage of fresh water in the islands.

Ground Water Resources

The geography of Andaman & Nicobar Islands is such that there are difficulties in the development of ground water resources. Saline aquifers (the interior rock zones having water) are encountered at shaloow depths. The Central Ground Water Board (CGWB) has undertakne systematic hydrological surveys, and 11promising sites bearing fresh water were pin-pointed in the South Andaman Islands. The surveys have revealed that shallow dug wells in the sandstones of South Andaman are capable of yielding 300 to 400 cu.m. per day. Sparing, emanating from the sandstones and volcanic rocks also have an average yield of 10 to 15 (liters) per minute during the lean season. In some places CGWB has succeeded in drilling tube wells. The well, dug in the God Alaikaddal Ayyanar campus with medium depth, gives very good drinking water. People of surrounding areas take water from the well. In order to provide water to the whole population of these islands, it is essential to have conjuncture use of surface and ground water resources.

Andaman & Nicobar Islands is abound in forest wealth. The forest are the main source of the territory's revenue and the major basis of its economy. The only industry worth the name found ther is wood based industry. The forests provide adequate variety and quantity of trees. Some high quality hardwood trees, which are scarce or not seen in the mainland, are found in these islands in abundance. The Padauk trees, whose value as raw material for furniture is invaluable, are common in these islands. The forest area of this territory is 7,171 sq. kms. Which is about 86% of the total land area of Andaman & Nicobar Islands. It is to be appreciated that whereas India as a whole has only 22.9% of its geographical area under forests, Andaman & Nicobar Islands has nearly four times that of national average (86.41%. This comprises 3,059 sq.kms. of reserve forests and 17 sq. kms. of protected forests and 4,112 sq.kms. for proposed reserve forests.

The forest of Andaman & Nicobar Islands are unique in character and possess enormous biological diversity. Of the 2,200 rare species of trees found in Andaman & Nicobar Islands, about 200 species : (10%) are endemic to these islands, but are found in Malaysis, Bruma, Indonesia and Polynesian islands, but are found in Malaysia, forests have been classified by Champin and Seth into the following groups:

Tidal Swamp Forest (mangrove forests)

Littoral Forests

Andaman Most Deciduous Forests

Andaman semi Evergreen Forests

Bamboo brakes

Cane Brakes

Southern Hilltop Tropical Evergreen Forests

Andaman Tropical Evergreen Forests and

Giant Evergreen Forests

The distribution and extent of each type of forest depends primarily on the climatic and topographic factors. The forest Department has made an assessment of the wood potential of these islands. It is estimated that about 3.63 lakhs cu.m. of different varieties of wood which includes 1,67,00 cu.m. of wood for plywood, 1,121,00 cu.m. of hardwood and 75,00 cu.m. of softwood will be available on a sustained basis.

PLANTATION RESOURCES

Plantation resources of Andaman & Nicobar Islands include coconut, arecanut, rubber, red oil palm and other plantations like cashew nut, nutmeg, cinnamon etc. which are discussed below.

Coconut

The location of these islands in the tropical belt and the high amount of rainfall provide favourbale conditions for the natural growth of coconut plants. The area under coconut cultivation in these islands is about 22,000 hectares with a production of about 7.3 crore of nuts per annum. The plantations are owned either by individuals o by cooperatives and are mostly concentrated in the islands of the Nicobar district Despite heavy consumption of coconut by the Nicobarese, the bulk of the production is sent to the mainland. Nearly 2020 hectares of Andaman & Nicobar Islands are under arecanut plantation with a production of about 3030 tons per annum. Arecanut is grown both in the Andaman as well as in the Nicobars. The Nicobar Group of Island accounts for the bulk of the areas as well as the production Arecanut is mainly sent to the mainland.

Rubber

The Rubber board made an assessment in the year 1959 that about 4000 hectares in Katchal, 1200 hectares in Ruthland and about 2400 hectares in Great Nicobar, could be brought under rubber plantation. The soil as well as the agro-climatic conditions in the territory, particularly in the Nicobar Group of Islands, are suitable for the introduction of rubber plantation on a large scale. At present, rubber plantation has been taken up in the South Andaman Group of Islands and Katchal Island of the Nicobar Group of Islands. In South Andaman, plantations were raised on revenue lands whereas in Katchal Island, the forest lands were utilized for this purpose. So far, an area of 614 hectares has been covered, out of which 593 hectares belongs to the

Rubber Board. Latex, a product form the rubber plantations is tapped. It is converted into rubber sheets and the entire production is sent to the mainland.

Red Oil Palm

The Forest Department initiated, on an experimental basis, red oil palm cultivation in Little Andaman in 1975 and covered an area of 2400 hectares. The area was, however, restricted to 200 hectares only under instructions from the Govt. of India pending study with regard to the effect of red oil palm plantations on the environment and ecology of these Islands. The experiment was subsequently taken over by the Forest Plantation Development Corporation Ltd., which started functioning from 1st April, 1977. About 1600 hectares of area has been planted so far. The red oil palm plantation involves clear felling of the rain forest.

Other Plantations

The other plantation crops like pepper, nutmeg, cashew nut, cinnamon etc., are being tried on an experimental basis in South Andaman. Pepper, cloves and cashew nuts are showing encouraging results.

Mineral Resources

In Andaman & Nicobar Islands, the mineral resources are very limited Chromium, copper, iron, silver, coal, limestone, oil and gas are the mineral resources found in the Islands. But no important deposit of any mineral has bene found. Exploratory activities of the ONGC in Andaman & Nicobar Islands were conducted in 1959 when geological surveys were started in the on-land area, followed by geophysical surveys in the off-shore areas. The first exploratory well AN-1, located in diligent Strait area, was drilled in 1980, and gas was extracted. Three more wells, drilled on the same geological structure, proved dry. Two more prospects (AN-21) in the western off-shore and AN-3-1 to the east of Ritchies Archipelago were also drilled. Thus a total of six wells were drilled in three prospects. At present, one is operating the Andaman off-shore area. As per the planning Commission, 1986 projected production of gas in Andaman & Nicobar Islands was 70 MMT in 1985-90 and 2230 to 4310 MMT in 1990-2000, where the projected production of oil is 1.22 to 1.45 MMT in 1990-2000.

Livestock Resources

The livestock of these islands consist mainly of cattle buffaloes, goats, poultry and pigs. Initially, all the livestock farming except rearing of pigs was undertaken to meet the requirements of the human population of these islands. Only very recently rearing of goats, buffaloes and poultry was started.

Marine Resources

The deep sea around Andaman & Nicobar Islands, the numerous inlets, bays and creeks are the abode of marine resources. With the declaration of 200 miles beyond the coast-line as our Economic Zone, Andaman & Nicobar Islands has a vast area around it for exploitation of the untapped marine resources. On the western side, the entire 200 miles extent can be explored. On the other three sides, Andaman & Nicobar Islands has to equally share the sea space with the neighboring countries. Various assessments were made in the past by the Indian experts on the availability of marine resources in the seas, surrounding the Andaman & Nicobar Islands, but no systematic study has so far been made to know the actual quantum of resources available for utilization. On this basis, the total net weight of the resources available is estimated to be about 1.07 million tones. The marine resources of Andaman & Nicobar Islands may broadly be divided into two groups as fish and shell.

Fish

It has been estimated that an area of 1,19,600 sq. miles around these islands has potential for fishing. The assessed fisher resources in these area is between 5 to 10 lakhs tones of fish per annum. But it is reported that the present catch in these islands is only 9692 tonnes. This clearly indicates that there exists a vast scope for the development, exploitation and utilization of the fish resources of these islands. Sardines and mackerels, the two important varieties of fish, are found towards the shore and can be exploited by the small boats using pursesuines and other nets. The entire region is full of sharks. The rocky bottom has great positional for percoid fishes (porches). According to a survey of marine resources conducted very recently by the Govt. of India Exploratory Fisheries Project and the Fisheries Department, it has come to light that a large number of varieties of fish having commercial value are available.

Three important species of the Tuna are found in the waters of Andaman & Nicobar Islands. They are (1) Skip jack (katusuwpnus pelamis) (2) Yellow fin (Tbunnus neothunnus) (albaesies macrpierus) (3) Big eye (Thunnus parathunnus (obus mebachi). A stock of 25000 tonnes of yellow fin and big eye in the sea around Andaman & Nicobar Islands has been estimated. About 50,000 tonnes of skip jack is also postulated for Andaman & Nicobar Islands. An item of commercial importance, found in plenty in the shallow waters around the main islands, is the seaslug or beach-de-mer (Holothurian). Out of nearly 40 species available, six species are of high commercial value which could yield substantial foreign exchange. About a dozen species of prawns are also found in these waters.

Shell

Andaman & Nicobar Islands is on abode of innumerable species of shells of various shapes and colours. Some of them have very high commercial value and many others form excellent show pieces. Turbo and Troches, the two species having high commercial value, are collected in plenty and are sent / exported to the mainland. The shells are used as raw materials in the Shell Handicraft Industrial Units which is a growing sector. The Fancy articles like necklace, bracelets, lamp shades and other ornaments are manufactured by the units. These items attract both domestic and foreign tourists. Besides the shells, five finger chanks, sacred chanks, pearly oysters, mussels, clams, cowries and numerous other varieties of high value and gastropod shells are found all along the shores. Their flesh is generally tasty and some are delicious. One more evidence to show the abundance of the marine resources is the apprehension of the foreign vessels by the Coast Guard, Navy and Police Department when they entered the coastal area of Andaman & Nicobar Islands for fishing.

Land Resources

The total land area of Andaman & Nicobar Islands is 8293 sq. kms. Out of which the Andaman Group of Islands covers an area of 6340 sq. kms. The available land resources of any country exercise a lasting effect on the economic life of man or nation because the production of raw material depends greatly on the nature of landscapes. In the hilly tracts, agriculture and industry generally cannot flourish. The result is that the production of wealth in these tracts is less and therefore, only a sparse population can be supported. In Andaman Islands, the available land resources are being utilized.

ECONOMY

The economy of Andaman & Nicobar Islands consists of agriculture, trade, commerce and industry. At present, very little quantity of paddy, sugarcane, banana, sweet potato, papaya, rabi pulse and vegetables are cultivated. Among the Andaman cash crops namely cashewnut, coconut, arecanut are grown. The last two are actively cultivated but the cashew nut is not taken seriously by the people of Andaman's. Some other vegetable like tomato, potato, cabbage, onion, cauliflower, beans, carrot, green chilies etc. are brought from the mainland. As far as the trade and commerce is concerned all types of trade are dominated by the Tamilians and Panjabis. But they purchase things from the mainland only. However, the inter-islands traders purchase goods from the Port Blair's traders only. Though the wholesale and retail trades are common, the special type of trade namely "Govt. Order Supply" is very famous in these Islands. As far as the industry is concerned all types of industries are found in Andaman & Nicobar Islands. But majority of the industrial units are based on wood. They satisfy the tourist with their handcrafts. Major portion of the cash inflow is from the budget allocation by the Central Govt. The status for the economy is not even developing but is at its infant stage with the full scope of growth and development. Tourism and industry are the only possible sectors in this territory which can develop the economy of the Andaman & Nicobar Islands.

3

Andaman Tribals

I had heard a lot about the tribes of Andaman and was really interested to observe their activities physically. While chatting at the residence of P.K. Subas who happened to be the Director, Doordarshan Port Blair those days, I had expressed my desire.

"No you can not do that?"

Why nobody is allowed to interact with them."

But why?

Subas in his late fourties was a matured and sincere officer. He had joined Port Blair in 2006 and took over a Director, Doordarshan. Lean and thin but tall gentleman was giving company to me and doctor during my stay at Port Blair. He was more conversant with the local laws and people of Andaman. Subas used to give us company in his official reservence where me and doctor used to visit normally on the weekends. Regular visitor of his residence was Jayarajan, working on Executive Engineer in Andaman Public works department. The reason for his visit was known to us.

For long looked upon with fear and fascination as a race of ferocious cannibals invested with the mystery that always surrounds the unknown, the autochthonous people of the Andaman and Nicobar islands became, when they were discovered in 1789 after the British occupation of the Islands, a major object of ethnographic interest and study. Their own legends begin with descriptions of a cataclysm which changd their entire history, and geologists understand this to be the series of volcanic eruptions that depressed some portions of the chain of islands in the bay of Bengal, notably those that linked it with the mainland of Asia, leaving above the water level an irregular and isolated string quite cut off from the rest of the continent. While ohers of their ilk on the mainland intermingled, progressed, and slowly evolved, they isolated, afraid of strangers, and defensively hostile to any incursion of exogenous influence, remained trapped in space and time. Evidence from their kitchen middens, which are old enough for the remais at the bottom to have fossilized, dated by some anthropologists to the Paleolithic or even the pre-lithic age, reveals that these autochthonous people have made little, if any, change in their lifestyle or food habits over the ecentures. Pretty much the same shells and bones, in about the same densities, have been found fossilized at the bottom of the middens as near the top, recently deposited. So old are they, infact,that some anthropologists have, on anatomical grounds, called them unique. The majority subscribes to the theory that they are Negritoes, linked, at some distant point in time, not to the Negroes or even the pygmies of Central Africa, but the Aetas of the Philippines and the Semange of the Malaysian Peninsula. Where as the Aetas and the Semange admitted other influences and adapted to other styles, the Andaman autochthons remain the pure representation of the original tribe, an example of how man lived before the advent of the stone age.

The inhabitants of the Andaman Islands are racially similar, but distinct, tribes, who over the years, due to geographical detachment and their own rudimentary skills at managing their environment, grew isolated from one another and, in a manner well documented by anthropologists, forgot their earlier associatios and affinities, and as languages evolved and changed differently, eventually lost even the ability to communicate with one another. In the nineteenth century, records maintained mainly by British officers with meticulous attention, show the existence of twelve tribes, each with its distinct territory, jealously guarded from the encroachments and depredations of the others, and distinct language. These twelve, or perhaps thirteen as later anthropologists have classified them, are listed in Table 3.1, along with the territories they occupied when the Islands were colonized, and the traditional tribal names for them.

He could go anywhere for liquor. One day doctor told him "You also contribute. What is this?"

"Are you Serious"? The reply came. We know the characters of Thirujan. He never used to take anything seriously.

Listen what I am singing? Jairajan used to start. His mother tongue was Malayali but he was having command own his voice. He had good collection of Hindi songs and could be found singing in his peculiar voice. He was a regular walker and covering a distance of eight to ten kilometer was was his routine.

"Anyway – told Subash

"These tribes are protected species and the administration is very much concerned about them.

"Jeevan se Bhari teri Akheyen – majboor kare jine ke liye – jine ke liye" — It was Jairajan. He was singing with a cigarette in his hand. Subash stated him but he was unmindful.

"Let me tell you the facts- "It was doctor. Actually the number of tribes have reduced once the years. The administration does not want to bring them with the contact of public. The Jarwas in contact with moden people have picked up the habit of chewing tobacos. Earlier the govt. used to provide coconut and bananas.

There was a protect from the sociologists. The argument was that they servived over the years with the support of administration. Don't bring them close to modern world or else they may be lossed their originality. There is a separate department of administration working for them Adim Janjati Vibhag.' In addition to them only doctors are allowed to interact.

Doctor went on telling. In case of need they contact the govt. people and come to the hospital alongwith their clain may be ten to fifteen in number. Cloth and food are provided to them by administration. After the treatment is over they go back to jungle. Before disappreciating they throw the clothes provided to them by the administration. They survive on honey and pigs. They but avoid killing the pregnant pigs. Normally the Jarwas do not stay at one place for long. They change their reservence.

One good thing which was noticed that immediately after pregnancy they come to the hospital and the doctor are able to save their child. Earlier they used to avoid consultation with the doctors during pregnancy period and after wards. Consequently, the infacts used to die. Jarwas were also not friendly earlier. Once a lad got his leg broken during police firing and he was admitted to hospital. He was treated and during his stay he learnt Hindi. After treatment he retired to Jungle and gave the masage that common people are not against them and as such not their enemy. This worked a lot and now-a-days they are not harming anybody what they used to do earlier.

"Tell me about other tribes-."

"I was telling you about the Jarwas. I have spent time with these people." Doctor continued and explained to me about the other tribes of Andaman and Nicobar Islands.

The aboriginals or the tribals of the Andaman Islands are known as Andaman Tribals. They are of Negrito stock/race. Their main occupation is food gathering. Andaman tribals are of four types namely :

1. Jarawas
2. Sentinalese

3. Onges and
4. Great Andamanese

After six months of my stay at Port Blair, I got an opportunity to meet my family in the mainland. I was a forced bachelor and as a matter of fact did never get opportunity to leave without family. It was a peculiar experience.

The concept of family can be well understood and you feel like living in a solitary confinement. I reached that "truly – Man is a social animal." Jails are nothing but solitary confinement. You need not be kept in any designated building. Your own place of stay becomes a Jail. You are alone and nothing else. Your monuments are not confined but you are in an open jail. You wait for the cry of the children, the advise of your life, the blessings of your parents, the laughter of the friends. Combined together a house is made, a concept of life develops and that can not be substituted. I was having all facilities at Port Blair- minus above and my conforts were of no use. The services of Prasad, my domestic help, Swamy and Grewal - and in addition to that other facilities – What not was there except family. I was staying along in the true sense of the term.

Time and tide waits for non. I had heard this but was feeling it in real life. My return journey was always painful. I used to feel the aircraft was searching me "Come I will drop you to Port-Blair."

I had to cut short my leave because of some vigent work at Rangit and accordingly. I returned to Port Blair. We had started for Rangit in a Tata sumo and besides Grewal Doctor was also acccompaning me . We had to be the part of first convoy which was to leave Thirgatang at 7.30. It takes 40-45 minutes from Port Blair to reach Thirgatang and Check- Post of Andaman Police.

Why the Police is manning this Check Post?

"We will be crossing the Jarwa reserve forest and private vehicle are not allowed to go without the permission of the administration. We crossed through the dense forest till we arrived Baratang. It was a small place. Doctor had made arrangement at the APWD Guest house. Tourists are regularly visiting this area on the pretext of seeing mud volcanos and lime cave. Jarwas are also visible on pockets while crossing this area. They come on the road in groups but the tourists or even the local people are not allowed to interact with them.

In the evening we arrived Rangat and stayed at the beautiful Guest house of APWD at the top of the hill. Rangat is a small township within a radian of around two kilometers. It can be accessed both by ship and road. Speed boats are operating regularly from Port Blair once daily and returning back on the same evening. There is a regular bus service from Port Blair. The journey takes around 6 hrs. Normally tourists are not coming and the only place to stay is the guest house under the control of APWD. Food is also a problem in this island. Snacks can be had from the local market.

Jarawas

Among the four tribals, Jarawas are forest dwellers and hostile. They inhabit and live in the west coast of South and Middle Andamans in the reserved forest area. They are claimed to be one of the purest and most primitive races in the world with a human memory "who live on hunting and food gathering". The jarawas do not have any relation with the other types of tribal and non-tribals and that's why nothing is known about their life style and economy, habits and characterizes. They look dark like other Negrito tribes and have thick skin and long but curly hair. Both the males and females are tall. It is understood that they love deers and like red colour. They do not wear dresses of any type. But they wear necklace, big mala waist bands, had bands made out of sea-shells, palm leaves and some bones. Sometimes they decorate their body with clay. They collect fruit honey, tuber from different plants fish monitor lizard, wild pig etc., for their food. But there is no evidence that they have killed deer and birds who are very friendly with jarawas. Till 1973, the Jaraws could not be contacted. In 1974, the Andaman & Nicobar Administration, with the joint efforts of Anthropology Department, succesfully contacted one groups of Jarawas and presented them gifts. From 1974 onwards, at irregular intervals, the Andaman & Nicobar Administration has been contacting the Jaraws and presenting them gifts, in the form of coconuts, red colured clothes, drinking water, other eatables etc. No attempt, however, has been made to stay with them because the behaviour of the Jaraws is still unpredictable.

Sentinalese

The Sentinalese are also forest dwellers and are very hostile. They are unapproachable. They inhabit and live in the isolated island named North Sentinal Island, situated in the west direction to the Port Blair. The Sentinalese are left alone in the reserved small island, the area of which is about 50 sq. kms. During the years 1967, 1978, 1982, 1984-1989, frequent attempts have been made to contact them by the Anthropological departments. But the last one was fairly successful in which the Sentinalese fleet free to come close to the Ventures boat in their (Sentinalese) canoes to pick up the gifts of coconuts which were floated by the ventures in the sea. The Sentinalese live in small sized huts under the trees. They use arrow and bow, plucking stick, arrow cum spear, bamboo pot, nautilus shells, fishing net, cane basket, waist band, grinding stone, hammer stone, resin, pig skull, dug out canoe, multi-pronged wooden harpoon spear etc. to serve their different ends.

Onges

Onges are a friendly tribe among the four Negrito tribes. They inhabit and live in the Little Andaman Islands and come in contact with outside civilization, following the setting up of the settlement. They are very friendly with the non tribals,. Occasionally, they come out of their residence or islands. "They are of dark colour, short statured with unusual growth of buttocks (both males and females). Their hands and feet are small but strong. Their eyes are bright and clear with in contrast to their complexion. Their teeth are remarkably strong and are retained till old age though not regularly cleaned". Most of the Onges are very weak and some of them suffer from a disease like tuberculosis. Now the Andaman & Nicobar Administration has opened a dispensary and individual health cards are being maintained. The local administration has constructed some modern double storeyed residential houses for them. They call themselves "Onges" a verbal noun meaning of "Man Being".

Great Andamanese

Great Andamanese are also one of the Andaman tribes like Negrito race. Once they dominated the full South Andaman islands with an estimated population of 5000 but due to the ill-treatment by the authorities in different years their strength has come down to 26 as per 1981 census. The main reason for this is that they have been contacted by the non tribals. "Great Andamanese were enjoying a free, independent and healthy life, free from disease. But the contact with the outside world brought epidemics like cholera, small pox, measles and contagious diseases like T.B, V.D etc." Great Andamanese are short in height. The colour of their skin is light black. Now–a-days they have started wearing all types of dresses including "T' shirts, available in the market.

NICOBAR TRIBALS

The aboriginals or the tribals of the Nicobar Islands are known as Nicobar Tribals. They are completely different from Andaman Tribals. Their main occupation is also food gathering.

Nicobar Tribals are of two types namely, Nicobaries and Shompens.

Nicobarese

Among the tribal population of Andaman & Nicobar islands, the Nicobarese are the advanced and most civilized and developing tribe. They wear good dresses and use cosmetics to beat par with the non tribals. They love one another and non tribals as well. Now-a-days, they get on employment in almost all the government jobs. They are very free and frank without any cunningness like others. Even they have started marrying the non tribals particularly mainlanders. They inhabit and live almost in all the parts of Nicobar group of islands. Nicobarese are also known as Holchu, living in fairly well organized communities. According to 1981 census their population was 21,727. Most of the Nicobarese are living in Car Nicobar and to a less extent in Nancowry and Katchal. Estimated and actual population is given in the Table 3.1. Their population nearly doubled in 80 years (1901-1981). On the basis of locality they live in, the Nicobarese can be divided into six tribes as given below:

Name	Locality
1. Car Nicobarese	Car Nicobar
2. Chowrite (Chowre Nicobarese)	Chowra
3. Teressan (Teresse Nicobarese)	Teressa and Bompokka
4. South Nicobarese	Pilowmillow Little Nicoabr etc.
5. Central Nicobarese	Nancowry, Kamorta, Trinket, and Katchal
6. Shompens	Interior places of Great Nicobar

Shompens

Another type of primitive tribes of Nicobar tribals is the Shompens. They inhabit the Great Nicobar Island. They are not like Jarawas, Sentinalese, Ongese or Great Andamanese who belong to Negrito race. But Shompens are from Mongoloid face. They live in interior jungles and feel very shy to come in front of any human being who is not of their race. They eat coconuts, bananas, pandanus, tubers, fish, wild pig, lizards etc. The Shompens do have some business relations with the Nicobarese. With the help of Yatrik (a department of Govt. of India) the local Administration has constructed some infrastructural facilities and helps the Shompens to lead a peaceful life. Andaman & Nicobar Administration has opened a school in their area to give formal and informal education. As per the records, their population is increasing.

There are four groups of indigenous tribes in the Andamans and two in the Nicobars. Their populations are generally showing declining trends except that of the Nicobarese, who are well assimilated into the mainstream. A comparative table of the populations of various tribes is given in Table 4.

The Great Andamanese are confined to Strait Island. The Onge are under constant disturbance from poachers and settlers in Little Andaman Island. The Sentinelese, still hostile, are undisturbed. However fishermen and lobster divers have been observed very close to coastline and inside bays of this island. This may be keeping the Sentinelese away from foraging in the intertidal reefs during low tide and from fishing out at sea in their dugout canoes (Andrews, per. Observ.)

The fourth tribe, the Jarawa, typify the debate ongoing in the islands. They were hostile until five years ago. Recent shedding of hostility has resulted in frequent contacts with settlers and passengers along the Andaman Trunk Road (ATR). The administration is taking action to reduce the contacts.

One school of thought believes that it is necessary to enable the Jarawa to abandon their forest existence and bring the benefits of "civilization" to them. Opposed to this is the vies that they should be left strictly alone; otherwise they will become extinct.

Supporting the latter view are the case histories of what happened to the Andamanese and the Onge tribes (Portman, 1899).

The Government of India has recently finalized its policy on the Jarawas. The objectives of the policy are (i) to protect the Jarawas from the harmful effects of exposure and contact with the outside world while they are not physically, socially and culturally prepared for such an interface, (ii) to preserve the social organization, mode of subsistence and cultural identity of the Jarawa community, (iii) to provide medical help to the Jarawas to reduce mortality and morbidity in case of their sudden affliction with diseases, which their systems are unaccustomed to; (iv) to conserve the ecology and environment of the Jarawa Reserve Territory and strengthen the support systems in order to enable the Jarawas pursue their traditional modes of subsistence and way of life, and (v) to sensitise the settler communities around the Jarawa habitat and personnel working for the protection and preservation of the Jarawas about the need to preserve this ancient community and to value their unique culture and lifestyle. With the said objectives in view, the Government of India has framed various strategies and guidelines for the protection and welfare of the Jarawas. The strategies include (a) protection of cultural identity by a policy of maximum autonomy to Jarawas with minimum and regulated intervention by the Government, (b) protectionof the natural habitat with no exploitation of natural resources within the tribal reserve and a ban on interaction between tourists and the Jarawas, (c) protection of health status by a periodic health surveys and extension of medical assistance in the Jarawa area itself, (d) regulation of traffic on the ATR by limiting it to the essential purposes of public transport, supplies and emergency evacuation of patients with movement only during restricted hours and in convoys, (e) Codification of the Jarawa language, so that the officials of the Administration, who are required to come in contact with the Jarawas, are able to communicate with them and understand their perception, reactions and problems, and (f) suitable institutional arrangements for the protection and welfare of all the aboriginal tribes including the Jarawas.

The recent order of the Supreme Court is to close the ATR in the section passing through the Jarawa Triabal Reserve, but the Andaman & Nicobar Administration has approached the Court for modification of the Order.

Also at stake here are the largest relatively undisturbed tracts of forests within the islands: the Jarawa Reserve, the Onge Reserve on Little Andaman Islands, and the Great Nicobar Biosphere Reserve, which acts as a home to the majority of the Shompen. Assimilation of the tribes into the mainstream is likely to increase pressure on the lands within the reserve for logging and encroachment, as well as increase in poaching activies.

In the evening we arrived Rangat and stayed at the beautiful Guest house of APWD at the top of the hill. Rangat is a small township within a radian of around two kilometers. It can be accessed both by shop and road. Speed boats are operating regularly from Port Blair once daily and retuning back on the same evening. There is a regular bus service from Port Blair. The journey takes around 6 hours. Normally tourists are not coming and the only place of stay is the guest house under the control of APWD. Food is also a problem in this island. Snacks can be had from the local market.

4

The Making of Cellular Jail

If you ask the name of any place worth visiting in Andaman, it was the Cellular Jail. It was my pleasure to visit it time and again. I was a regular visitor of G.B. Pant hospital and the Jail premises is standing in front of the road which goes to the hospital. I had a lot of discussion with local residents, Grewal, doctor and Subash whenever I got the opportunity. It is a tale of supreme sacrifice of the freedom fighters and in standing as a proof of valour and patriotism.

It was from Grewal I came to know that the building is being maintained by IP&T Department of Andaman administration. A light & sound programme is being organized on day to day basis in the evening. People visiting Andaman should not miss it.

Towards the end of the eighteenth century the British rulers in India were looking for a suitable site where they could establish a penal settlement for Indian convicts far away from Indian Manland beyond the seas. Such overseas penal settlements had already been established at Benkoelen, Malacca, Penang, Arakan, Tenasserim and Singapore.

On the recommendations of two explorers, who visited the Islands in 1789, Captain Archibald Blair, Hydrographer of the East India Company and Colonel R. H. Colebrrok, the Surveyor general of India, a convict colony associated with a harbour of refuge was set up at Catham Islands in 1790 and later on, at the instruction of Commodore Cornwallis, it was shifted to North Andaman. It was, however, abandoned in 1796 on account of unhealthy conditions and high mortality rate of the settlement.

The idea of re-establishing a penal settlement was germinated in the minds of the British rulers after the outbreak of the Great Indian Revolt – The First War of Independence in 1857. A large number of "Mutineers," "Deserters" and "Rebels" were arrested by the British. They were so large in number that the British rulers found it practically impossible to accommodate them in the Indian Jails or in the overseas penal settlements o South-East Asia. Such a situation forced the British rulers to seek a place to establish a penal settlement and Andaman islands came for active consideration.

An Andaman Committee was constituted by the government under the Presidentship of Dr. F.J. Mouat to explore the island for establishing the penal settlement. On the recommendations of the Committee a penal settlement was set up at Chatham Islands. Captain H. Man, the Jail Superintendent in Moulemin was sent to Port Blair to occupy formally the Islands. He hoisted the British flag on 22 January 1858 at Port Blair and thus marked the beginning of an unhappy chapter in the history due to which the Andaman Islands acquired the sinister name of Kalapani.

Even since the establishment of British rule in India, it met occasionally with resistance from local people under local leaders but all these resistance were confined to smaller areas. In May 1857 resistance of the Indian people assumed national character, covering the whole of the country all at one- time. A large number of prisoners in 1857-58 and subsequent years were convicted for their participation in the First War o Independence. These prisoners, sentenced to transportation on charges of waging war against the British government were sent in batches to Port Blair. Even as late as 1876, "Mutineers" of 1857 were sentenced to transportation.

Thus the First War of Independence supplied the first batch of prisoners in the Andamans. Unfortunately the number of "Mutineers of 1857" transported to the Andamans is not exactly known. However, this book brings to light for the first time more than 300 names of those who were sentenced to transportation to the Andamans along with the available records of the individual freedom fighters.

The Heroes of 1857 were subjected to soul crushing labour in hostile conditions and were whipped mercilessly for the slightest lapse by dr. J.P. Walker - the Superintendent of the penal settlement. A large number of them died in the Andamans unwept and unsung. A few of them were released after a long servitude and the rest after release, made the Islands their permanent abode.

The next group of prisoners in Andamans were Wahabis. Wahabi movement was started by a set of Muslims led by "Abdul Wahab Neijidi" of Saudi Arabia from whose name the movement came to be known as Wahabi movement. Gradually the movement became very strong under the leadership of Syed Ahmed Barailvi of Patna. After his death in 1831, his followers fought against the British from their base camp at Sitana. The movement was started against the ruthless system of land settlement by the British Government. A large number of Wahabis were tried and sentenced to transportation for life to the Andamans where they too passed through a life full of sufferings and tortures.

In later years, many companions of vasudev Balwant Phadke, the great revolutionary of Maharashtra were sentenced to transportation which was followed by the prisoners convicted in the Manipuri revolt of 1891. During the Anglo-Manipuri conflict of 1891, British officers were openly executed by the Manipuris. After the suppression of the revolt, the prisoners who were mainly responsible for the murder of British officers, were put on trial and either sentenced to death and executed or transported to the penal settlement in the Andamans. Shortly afterwards a large number of Burmese of Tharawadda, who revolted against the British, were also transported to Andamans.

In January 1890, C.J. Lyall and Surgeon Major A.S. Lethbridge were sent to Port Blair by the Government of India to look into the convict management at Port Blair. The report submitted by them in April 1890 revealed that the convicts preferred transportation to Port Blair to a stay in an Indian Jail. Hence they recommended that life of a convict in the penal settlement of Andamans should be more penal in character. Apart from giving other suggestions, they also recommended separate confinement for a period of 6 months after the arrival of a convict at Port Blair. Thus paved the way for the construction of the Cellular Jail, a huge building of red-brown bricks with long arms – three storeys in height- stretching from a common centre like the rays of a star fish provided 698 cells from solitary confinement. The Cellular Jail, today stands as a symbol of India's revolutionary struggle for freedom.

In the beginning of the twentieth century the Swadeshi movement, the partition of Bengal and the emergence of extremist group in the country led to the adoption of violent methods. Revolutionary activities grew up in Maharashtra, Bengal, Punjab and some other provinces. Anushilan Samiti was the most important organization which played a prominent role in planning and executing the attacks on British officials with headquarters in Bengal and branches in many parts of the country. Arms were collected and bombs were manufactured by them.

In Maharashtra the movement which began with Vasudev Balwant Phadke was carried on by Vinayak Damodar Savarkar. Most of the revolutionaries of Maharashtra were in association with the revolutionary society of Abhinav Bharat. Vinayak Damodar savarkar later became a comrade of Shyamjee Krishna Verma who founded the Indian Home Rule Society in London.

However the movement was not confined in India alone. The Indian revolutionaries realized the importance of setting up centres of agitation and propaganda in foreign countries. The Gadar movement launched by the Punjabi revolutionaries who were well- settled in various countries like Canada, America, Burma China and Japan is worth mentioning. They came to the country with a mission to wage the war against the British Empire in India. They were influenced by its ideology and patriotic fervour.

Above mentioned revolutionary activities supplied the political prisoners in the Cellular Jail. First in the series were the prisoners convicted in the Alipore Bomb Case. A few editors of Swarajya and other papers were also transported to the Cellular Jail from United Province for writing seditious articles. Savarkar brothers were sentenced to transportation and deported to the Cellular Jail in the Nasik Conspiracy Case. A large number of "Gadar Heroes" were convicted in Lahore Conspiracy Case and transported to the Cellular Jail. In subsequent years till 1921 a large number of revolutionaries from different parts of India and Burma were also sent to the Andamans.

The Jail officials in the Andamans adopted all possible methods to break the spirit of the political prisoners. The quantity of work given to them was impossible to complete in the fixed time. The food given to them was not only insufficient but also was of a very bad quality. Harsh treatment and humiliation by jail officials became a routine affair. As a result of sufferings and torture a large number of political prisoners fell ill, a few became insane and a few great sons courted martyrdom in the Cellular Jail.

In 1921 the Government of India proposed to abandon the Andamans as a penal settlement and accordingly most of the political prisoners were repatriated to the Indian Jail. Meanwhile Moplah revolt took place in 1921-22 in the Malabar region. A large number of Moplahs were arrested and deported to the

Andamans inspite of the government decision to close down the penal settlement in Andamans. Moplahs were initially confined in cellular Jail but later they were granted agricultural tickets and were allowed to bring their families from Malabar. During this period many Rumpa peasants from Andhra Pradesh were also transported to the Andamans. The Rumpa Peasants rebelled against the British government under the leadership of Alluri Sitaram Raju.

The proposal to close down the penal settlement received a further setback on account of a number of revolutionary movements in India. The most important revolutionary party of north India - The Hindustan Socialist Republican Association, organized revolutionary activities under great patriots namely Bhagat Singh, Sukhdev, Rajguru and Batukeshwar Dutt. From 1925-1929 members of this organisation were sentenced and arrested in the Lahore Conspiracy Case. 7 members of the party were also transported to the Andamans. In 1930 occurred the most powerful revolutionary activity against the British – Chittagong Armoury Raid in Bengal in which nearly 100 youths participated and there were many casualties on both sides.

Under the circumstances the government of India reopened the penal settlement in the Andamans in 1932. the prisoners convicted in Chittagong Armoury Raid Case, Lahore Conspiracy Case and a number of other revolutionaries were sent to Cellular Jail with long term sentences.

New political prisoners of the Cellular Jail resorted to hunger strike in January 1933 against the inhuman treatment by the Jail staff and poor living conditions. Later, on the assurance of the Chief Commissioner to look into their problems, the political prisoners agreed to call off the strike. On seeing that the Government is not at all bothered about their sufferings and demands, the inmates of Cellular Jail went again on hunger strike on 12 May 1933 which was followed by customary method of force feeding. As a result of brutal force feeding process Mahavir

Singh, Mohit Moitra and Mohan Kishore Namadas died one after other. The martyrdom of three political prisoners caused strong dissatisfaction and the Government of India was compelled to send Colonel Barker to the Andamans. Strike was called off after45 days as demands of the political prisoners were conceded by the Government.

The year 1937 was a turning point in the history of penal settlement when Congress decided to form ministers in seven provinces. This was followed by the demands of the political prisoners in the andamans which included immediate repatriation of all the political prisoners from the Andamans. The political prisoners also sent ultimatum to the Governemnt of India, "that unless be forced to resort to hunger strike."

The Governemnt was not much concerned with these demands of the political prisoners. Thus they decided to resort to hunger strike on 24 July 1937. At last, after 45 days the Government promised to repatriate the political prisoners. The last batch of political prisoners was repatriated on 18 January 1938.

But this was not an end to the sufferings of the free people of Andamans who were mostrly the descendants of convicts called "Local Born" and other free citizens of India and Burma who settled here with their families. Shortly after the repatriation of political prisoners from andamans, Second World War broke out in September 1939. After the Japanes invasion of Singapore and Burma, the invasion of Andaman & Nicobar was considered imminent in the next few days. The British Government on realizing that they did not posses enough military strength to safeguard this Bay Islands, decided to evacuate officers, their families and civilians who were ready to leave the Andamans. But along with few British and Indian officers, the local born population remained in the Islands.

The Japanes Imperial Force invaded the Islands on 23 March 1942. They were very quiet and friendly to the people in the begininning but later they put to death many hundreds of people in the most barbaric way. Many of the educated persons who were mostly the members of Indian Independence League branch at Port Blair were rounded up as suspected spies of the British and were incarcerated in the Cellular Jail. They were either shot dead by the Japanese or died due to prolonged tortures and sufferings. The Homfraygunj Martyrs Memorial today stands as a mute testimony to the barbaric tortures inflicted on the innocent people of Andamans.

Supreme Commander of I.N.A., Netaji Subhash Chandra Bose visited the Andaman Islands from 29 to 31 December 1943 after the historic declaration of the Japanese Prime Minsiter at the Greater East Asiatic Nation's Assmebly in Tokyo on 6 November 1943 that the Andaman & Nicobar Islands would be transferred to the Provisional government of Azad Hind. On 30 December 1943 Netaji hoisted the tricolour flag at Port Blair.

The Islands were captured by the British after the defeat of Japan in the Second World War, followed by the abolition of penal settlement in 1945 after 88 years since the first war of Indepemndence in 1857.

After independence, the freedom fighters who were incarcerated in the Cellular Jail formed on association called " Ex-Andaman Poltical Prisoners' fraternity Circle" which demanded the coversion of Cellular Jail into National memorial. The demand of the "Ex- Andaman Politcal Prisoners' Fraternity Circle" was accepted in principle by the Government in 1969. But formally the Cellular Jail was dedicated to the Nation on 11 February 1979 by the then Prime Minsiter of India, Shri Morarji Desai in the presence a large number of freedom fighters.

To day, three surviving wings of the National Memorial stand as a mute testimony to the glory of indomitable spirit of the heroes of India's revolutionary freedom struggle. Andamans in general and the Nationsal Memorial - Cellular Jail in particular will serve as a beacon light to many generations inspiring them to dedicate themselves in order to give a new meaning and content to out freedom.

Another two wings of the jail were demolished after India achieved independence. However, this led to protests from several former prisoners and political leaders who saw it as a way of erasing the tangible evidence of their persecution. The remaining three wings and the central tower were therefore converted into a National Memorial in 1969.

The Govind Ballabh Pant Hospital was set up in the premises of the Cellular Jail in 1963. It is now a 500-bed hospital with about 40 doctors serving the local population

The centenary of the jail's completion was marked on 10 March 2006: Many erstwhile prisoners were felicitated on this occasion by the Government of India

The main purpose of the Cellular Jail was the housing of 600 convicts in utter isolation. Humanity and rehabilitation of the convicts not being a concept that the British were familiar with, they came up with a diabolical plan that was successful beyond their wildest dreams. Indeed, just being incarcerated there, day in day out was enough to break the toughest spirit—the beatings, insults and excruciating hard labor crushed their soul. The Cellular Jail was divided into seven wings radiating out from a central core, called gomati—just like the spokes of a wheel. The wings were of unequal length and three storey in height. All drawings unless otherwise stated are schematic representations, drawn from memory and are not to scale.They were numbered from 1 to 7. A fifteen foot boundary wall enclosed the whole jail, touching each wing, creating self-contained units. The only exception was block. The gomati, though often given the misnomer tower, is just a center space in which all the wings opened out. It has a center seven-sided core with arched openings. The gomati has no staircase of its own.The ends of the wings near the gomati end are located so close to each other, from a distance they almost seem to meet. This gap between the two wings is the only way out of the triangular yards (except at the main entrance) that are formed between them. At ground level, each wing is accessed by narrow raised walkway @ plinth height (about 3') with steps on either side. At upper levels the center core has a passage around it, with connectors leading to the wings. The connectors are accessed by low wooden gates. At the end wall of each wing, on each level, is a barred door. This is the only exit from each wing (block 1 and 7 are exceptions, mentioned below). Beyond this gate is the staircase on the left. Block 7 has an additional gate beyond the staircase.The staircase of the wings do not go to the roof. Roof is accessed by a wooden staircase in the center of the gomati from the third storey. The gomati has one more level which has the bell. This is covered by a red-tiled roof held up bycolumns

Features of the Yard: Each triangle of yard formed between two wings was provided with a workshop, toilet block and a reservoir 15'long and 1 ½' wide for bathing purpose. Water was pumped into it from the sea. Fresh water for drinking was provided by pipes and some yards had wells. The only way out of the yard was through the gomati (except the main entrance)

Exterior is of exposed bricks, except at ground level where is it is plastered white. The front of each wing looked upon the back of the next—a blank wall with ventilators completely covered by awnings. Each wing is made up of rows of cells 13' x 7' in size. A wide (7' or 8', perhaps) passage runs in front of the cells. The front facade is a barred arched colonnade, enclosing this passage. Opening of each cell is centered on the arch of the façade. The passage was lit by lamps at both ends of the

The main entrance was in the center of wide plastered block painted golden-yellow, leading to an open area @ the ground level.Barred metal gates with doorway in the middle enclosed the open are at both ends. Short flights of steps lead to offices on both sides. The upper level of the entrance, which was the residence of the Jailor and Deputy Jailor, continued over this area. Apartments of all other officials connected with the jail were located outside, but near the main entrance. This entrance hall had walls decorated with all the manacles, fetters and weaponry, to awe the convicts. The façade had turrets, housing staircases on either side of the entrance.The boundary wall coming from block 2 and block 7 connects with the end walls of the entrance, closing the loop. Entering the yard, there was a peepal tree immediately in front. To the left was the hospital of 15 to 20 beds—razed to the ground now. The memorial flame is built upon its flame. Block 1, ending just before the hospital, housed some cells reserved for hospital use. Some of the barred arches of this block open into the yard—for easy access to hospital cells perhaps? To the right is the gallow house and kitchen.

The front of wall of the cell had a narrow (about 2') opening with a barred door set in the middle of an immensely thick wall. This severely restricted the convicts line of vision, especially with the wide passage before it. From many cells, especially those on the lower levels near the gomati the convict could see nothing except the blank wall. The back wall had a 3' x 2' high ventillator with a sill height of 10'. The sloped awning covering it was so deep only a sliver of light was visible at the bottom.There were no lamps provided in the cells, and with these meager openings it was almost perpetually bathed in gloom. The latch system was so designed, that the convict could not see it, nor ever hope to bend his armaround the thick wall.

Plans of Cell Section showing restricted line of vision Latch system of the cell. The darkness within in contrast to bright light without .

The story of Cellular Jail is not complete without Vir Savarkar. A freedom fighter with extreme determination and impregnable loyalty towards the nation, was the part of his personality. The Air port has rightly been named as Vir Savarkar. The Jail authorities also celebrate his birthday every year and the Cell where he was confined is still a centre of attraction.

Vinayak Damodar 'Veer' Savarkar is back in the news, 38 years after he passed into the ages. The late champion of Hindutva returned to the headlines when Petroleum Minister Mani Shankar Aiyar recently ordered the removal of a plaque with a message by Savarkar from the historical CellularJail on the Andaman and Nicobar Islands Aiyar also criticised Savarkar, leading to the Shiv Sena and Bharatiya Janata Party in Maharashtra demanding an apology from the Congress MP.

Savarkar (1883 to 1966) was a revolutionary who spent many years in prison in the Andamans. He propounded the philosophy of Hindutva and was linked to Mahatma Gandhi's assassination, but was not found guilty.

He was born on May 28, 1883, in Bhagpur village near Nashik. After his parents died young, his elder brother Ganesh looked after the family. In 1898, the British hanged the Chapekar brothers in Pune for killing a British officer. This had a deep impact on the teenaged Savarkar, who decided to take up armed struggle against the British. In 1901, he joined the Ferguson College in Pune and set up the Abhinav Bharat Society, which preached a revolutionary struggle against the British. He also won a scholarship that took him to Britain to study law in 1906.

In Britain, Savarkar organised students and advocated an armed struggle to throw the British out of India. He also wrote his book on the 1857 Sepoy Mutiny, which he called India's First War of Independence, a terminology the Indian government accepted after Independence. Since there was no question of printing the book in Britain, it was printed in Holland and copies of it were smuggled into India.

The book was a huge success, giving Indians a strong sense of pride, providing a fresh perspective on a war that was till then merely seen as the outcome of disgruntled Indian soldiers in the service of the British. The second edition was published by Indians in the US while Bhagat Singh printed the third edition. Its translations were a big success: the Punjabi and Urdu translations travelled far and wide while the Tamil translation almost becoming mandatory reading for soldiers of Subhas Chandra Bose's Indian National Army — a majority of who were Tamilians from Southeast Asia.

In Britain, he also created a network of like-minded individuals. Given his anti-British activities, the police soon came looking for him. He was arrested in London on March 13, 1910 and sent to India to face trial.

The story that made Savarkar a national hero! The ship in which he was being taken to India berthed at Marseilles, France, on July 8, 1910. Savarkar wriggled out of the porthole and swam a great distance in the cold water to reach the shore. He had earlier told his friends, including Madame Bhikaji Cama, to meet him at Marseilles, but they arrived late and the British recaptured him. Since Savarkar did not speak French, he was unable to tell the local policeman that he was a refugee. Even though he could not escape, this story resonated across India.

He was tried, and on December 24, 1910, sentenced to 50 years in prison. On July 4, 1911, he was sent to Port Blair's Cellular Jail.

Savarkar's supporters always point to his incredibly difficult and degrading days in jail, sentenced to rigorous imprisonment when he was in the prime of life; placed in solitary confinement while other leaders had it much easier and were released whenever their health failed or someone in the family fell ill. Savarkar enjoyed no such luxury.

In 1920, Vithalbhai Patel, Vallabhbhai Patel's elder brother, demanded Savarkar's release, a demand also backed by Gandhi and Nehru. On May 2, 1921, Savarkar was shifted from the Cellular Jail, first to the Alipore Jail in Bengal and then to Ratnagiri Jail in western Maharashtra. He was released on January 6, 1924 on the condition that he would not leave Ratnagiri district, which is not very far from Mumbai (then Bombay), till 1937.

Up to this point, most historians regardless of ideology would agree that Savarkar was a committed revolutionary, even if one does not support the notion of an armed struggle. But from the point of his release from jail, Savarkar becomes a divided figure, either loved or loathed. Savarkar agreed he would abstain from political activities to facilitate his release. His supporters say he only made such promises to get out of prison and that he remained committed to throwing the British out of India.

He became active in the Hindu Mahasabha, founded in 1915, which sought to protect the interests of Hindus. The Hindu Mahasabha, which differed radically from the Indian National Congress, attracted followers who were either opposed to Gandhi and the Congress, or believed in Hindutva.

Savarkar, who popularised the term 'First War of Independence', also coined the term Hindutva when he wrote an eponymous book. The book outlined the features of Hindutva, including its economic, social, and political aspects. He also wrote another book in English, Hindupadpadshahi, extolling the Maratha rule over India. He had developed and expounded the notion of one nation, one culture, bound by blood and race. In 1937, he became president of the Hindu Mahasabha, and remained in the post till 1943.

For his supporters, Savarkar believed in a strong Hindu society and in the Hindutva ideology of one nation, one culture, one people, which meant no special provisions for any minority. For his opponents, this ideology divides India today by trying to deny the minorities a rightful place in Indian society. As the bitter political battle over Aiyar's decision reveals, the controversy over Veer Savarkar's legacy is far from concluded

In the light of the Savarkar row and inconsequential discussions on the role of various personalities in the backdrop of freedom struggle, it is fit to introduce one of the most deserving freedom fighters of undivided India, who not only succeeded in his mission, but also sacrificed his life for his motherland.

Sher Ali Khan, 30 years of age, strong and well-built, son of Wali from a village near Jamrood, a Khyberee of Kookee Kheyl clan, and a resident of Pakhree in the Kabul territory, was convicted on the April 2, 1867 by Colonel Pollock, Commissioner of Peshawar and sentenced to transportation for life.

He reached Andaman Penal Settlement in May 1869 via Karachi and Bombay. No doubt can be cast on the character of this bold and gallant young man who had no history of any immoral act, except on one occasion, on which he had in his possession some flour for which he could not account.

Then followed a lengthy account of Lord Mayo's inspection tour of the Andaman Islands culminating in this description of the assassination:

After descending the hill the Lord safely reached the shore of Hope Town. But when they approached a carriage standing there, Chief Commissioner, with the permission of the Lord, stepped back for some urgent work while the Lord and Private Secretary kept on moving slowly.

At that time a person jumped like a tiger from behind the carriage and stabbed the Lord with his knife twice so sharply that Lord Mayo stumbled and fell into the sea.

The torch got extinguished in this confusion but another prisoner was brave enough to catch hold of the assassin, otherwise he would have killed some more people. Lord Mayo was taken out of the sea and was made to lie down in the carriage. After saying a few words Lord Mayo passed away.

When the assassin was asked why he did that, he said that he had done it on orders from God. Then he was asked, if there was any co-conspirator. He said: 'Yes, God is the co-conspirator.'

After investigation, in accordance with the laws of Bengal, death sentence was awarded to the assassin.

'Since 1869 I wanted to assassinate some high British official and that is why for several years I had been preparing this knife.

When Lord Mayo arrived on February 8, 1872 and salute was given to him, I sharpened my knife once again.

'The whole day I was looking for an opportunity to somehow reach an island where I could find him moving around. But I did not get the opportunity. In the evening when I had lost all hope, death brought the Lord to me. I accompanied the Lord on the mountain and came here too with him. But while going as well as while coming back I didn't get a chance. Then I came and hid myself behind the carriage. My long cherished desire was fulfilled only here.'

Although old and short, he was a strong and brave man. Even then till the date of his hanging he was never upset. While being hanged, he loudly addressed the prisoners: 'Brothers! I have killed your enemy and you are a witness that I am a Muslim.' And then he breathed his last while reciting Kalima.

This incident, i.e. the assassination of Lord Mayo by an ordinary prisoner is an example of divine power. Otherwise how can an ordinary person like Sher Ali match with a powerful person like Lord Mayo, the Governor General.

When the death arrived, all the guards wearing swords as well as armed police, precautions and arrangements were of no use. God does the things the way He wants and no one can alter that: this was the remark made by several people.

The incident shocked the British Empire. It was not ready to accept any explanations. Hence, the trial that happened onboard Glasgow, a steam ship, would go down in history as the speediest trial ever.

On February 16, the Calcutta Appellate Court confirmed the death sentence and on February 21, the Calcutta High Court put its seal on the verdict. A copy of the verdict was dispatched to Andamans by Scotia, a steamboat and reached here on February 27. On March 11, 1872, the great son of the undivided India was hanged to death at the Viper Gang Jail.

I always used to remember what was the concept behind the word 'kalapani'. It was only a reflection of the nefarious designs, in thoughts and pre conceived ideas of the British who never cared for the human rights or even the personal liberties. Here in the Cellular Jail is written the misdeeds and too centiments of a human race who had come to this country to rule and to crush all the heads who dared to speak against them. It was indifferent concept of life which dominated the rulers but could not gain anything for them except hatred which ultimately set their departure and made this place immortal in the anuls of history.

I do not know to what extent these facts and would sustain the litmus test of historical researches. I have just tried to reduce the storm I could hear in Andaman about these personalities.

These stories never the less are lessons for the people who are against the communal harmony. My information produced here is gathered from the Andamaneese hearsay and from some published materials, I am sure in any form it will not reflect adversely to any individual or to the martyr's prestige so that I may be remarked with any individuals posture of caste and creed.

5

Andman and Freedom Struggle

A question always haunted in my mind as to being the integral part of India since long, how these islands could remain unaffected by the Indian national movement. This is an unfortunate chapter of our history also that the students of History are not taught about this events and the knowledge on this aspect especially to the mainlanders is far from appreciable. Like the residents of Andaman many people who contributed a lot during the war of independence remained unsung heroes. No efforts seems to be taken by the Historian to know and write about them.

One day I asked Grewal "Are you aware whether anybody from these islands ever participated in the war of Independence or against the foreign rule."

Why not Sir. Many people are there. A few who were incarcerated in the cellular jail are still alive. It was quite surprising. When we talk about the freedom struggle, we talk about the people of mainland only and definitely there is no mention of the people living in these islands. When we talk about the Cellular Jail, it reminds us about the people who were deported from the mainland to the Cellular Jail.

I really wanted to meet them? Can you help me?

Grewal was also inclined to help me. He also seemed to be interested in this subject.

"Meanwhile I will give you book published by the Directorate of Youth Affairs, Sports and Culture Andaman and Nicobar Administration Port Blair.

Grewal had Graduatedfrom Delhi University. Being a student of history - I was unaware of any such publication.

Were you a student of history?

'No Sir – not at all.'

The other day the book was in my hand. "Unsung Heros of freedom struggle in Andaman 'who's who.' The book was compiled and edited by Rashida Iqubal. This book was published by Far Sight Publishers and distributers S – 16. Naveen Sahdara Delhi in 2004.

In this book, details are available regarding a number of persons who were the residents of Andaman and Nicobar and were victimized by the Japanese during Japanese occupation of the island in 1942-45.

Records regarding following persons are available in this book

Abdul Jalil : Born on 15 February 1910, son of Nazeer Mohd, residence Aberdeen bazaar, Port Blair, Andamans. Arrested by the Japanese Imperial Force in October 1943. Imprisoned in the Cellular Jail. Faced torture in the Jail. Killed by the Japanese Firing Squad on 30 January 1944 and buried at Homfraygunj, Andamans.

Abdul Khalique : Born on 26 August 1921, son of M. Abdul Rauf, residence Aberdeen Bazaar, Port Blair, andamans. Joined the Indian Independence League at Port Blair. Arrested by the Japanese Imperial Forces on 22 January 1943. Kept in the Cellular Jail. On 30 March 1943 shot dead by the Japanese Firing Squad near Dugnabad shore.

Anant Lall : Belonged to Rohtak, Haryana. Deported to the Cellular Jail on transportation for life. After relese, became a member of Indian imdependence League. Arrested in OPctober 1943 in 2nd spy case by the Japanese Force. Shot dead and buried on 30 January 1944 at Homfraygunj, Andamans.

Attar Singh : Born in 1907, son of Gonan singh, residence Pahargaon, south andamans. Japanese Imperial Force suspected him as a spy of the British. Arrested on 22 January 1943 in the 1st spy case. Kept in the 6th wing of Cellular Jail. Shot dead by the Japanese force on 30 March 1943.

A.D. Scott : Wife of A.D. scott, assistant Commissioner of Nicobar, killed by the Japanese during 1942-1945.

Albert Robetson : Residence Mus village, tuhet chiang, soldier of British army, killed by the Japanese during 1942-45.

Alfred Joseph : Residence Mus village, tuhett Malako, murdered by the Japanese during 1942-45.

Ali Hussain Volimov Kutti : Residence chukchucha village, Tuhet Re-angtima, murdered by the Japanese.

Alik : Resoidence Amalacca village, tuhet Taichsa, killed by the Japanese during 1942-45.

Arthur Hongla : Residence Arong Village, tuhet pooto, murdered by the Japanese at tomamana arong during 1942-45.

Asulki : Residence Chukchucha Village, tuhet Hontom- sok, murdered by the Japanese.

Bachan Singh : Born on 12 April 1900, son of Nehal Singh, residence Rupar, Punjab. Joined the Indian Independence League during 1942. Arrested by the Japanese Imperial force. Kept in the cellular jail later shot dead and buried on 30 January 1944 at homfraygunj, andamans.

Bakshish Singh : Belonged to Punjab. Deserted from the Allied force during December 1943 in Andamans. Arested by the Japanese force. Shot dead and buried on 30 January 1944 at Homfraygunj, Andamans.

Balwant Singh : Belonged to Punjab. Deported to the cellular Jail on transportation for life. Arrested and confined in the Cellular Jail by the Japanese Imperial force during 1943. Shot dead and buried on 30 January 1944 at Homfraygunj, Andamans.

Banta Singh : Belonged to Punjab, sepoy no.3545 of Indian Military police, transferred to Andaman islands. Resided in Haddo. Arrested and confined in the Cellular Jail by the Japanese Imperial force. Shot dead and buried on 30 January 1944 at Homfraygunj, Andamans.

Basant Lal : Son of Bharat Lal, residence Junglighat, Port Blair, Andamans, Munshi in forest department.Tortured brutally, shot dead and buried on 30 January 1944 at Homfraygunj, Andamans.

Beg, Fazal : Belonged to united Province, deported to Andaman islands on transportation. Joined the Indian Independence League. Arrested and confined in the cellular jail, shot dead and burined on 30 january 1944 in a mass grave at homfraygunj.

Bhikam Singh : Born in 1914, son of ganga ram, residence Bejnaur, united Province, Bhantu. Arrested along with his brother Malkhan Singh by the Japanese force. Confined in the Cellular Jail, faced inhuman torture. Died on 30 November 1943 in the Cellular Jail.

Charanji Lal : Born in 1918, son of Ganesha, residence Murshidabad, united Province. Arrested and detained in the Cellular Jail. Subjected to inhuman torture. Died on 21 January 1944 in Cellular Jail.

Chawla, Hil Singh : Son of trilok singh, residence Punjab. Deported oto the Andamans on life transportation. Donated a large sum of rupees for the cause of the League which was later donated to netaji Subhash Chandra Bose on 30 december 1943 at Port Blair. Arrested on 12 January 1944 and confined in the

Cellular Jail. Shot d ead and buried on 30 January 1944 at homfraygunj, Andamans.

Chawla, Kaur Singh : son of Bhagwan das, residence Punjab. Deported to andamans on transportation for life. Arrested on 12 January 1944 and kept in the Cellular Jail. Shot dead and buried on 30 January 1944 at homfraygunj.

Chawla, Pokhar Singh : Son of Sijjan Ram, residence Punjab. Arrested on 12 January 1944 by the Japanese force. Confined in the Cellular Jail, shot dead and buried on 30 January 1944 at Hommfraygunj.

Chotey Singh : Residence Punjab. Served at Port Blair as a Sepoy no. 2534 of the Indian Military Force.Arrested by the Japanese Force. Subjected to inhuman torture. Shot dead on 30 March 1943 at Dugnabad. His body was cremated by his colleagues.

Chirustu : Residence Small Lapati Village, tuhet Kafutngo, killed by the Japanese.

Choknya : Residence Malacca Village, tuhet Taichsa, killed by the Japanese.

Cho-On : Residence Malacca Village, tuhet Re-ang ıhong, killed by the Japanese.

Christopher : Residence Mus, Tuhet Tongmi, killed by the Japanese.

Cyril Job : Residence Mus Village, Hanoich, an employee of medical department at Kamorta island, killed by the Japanese.

Dalip Singh : Residence Punjab, deported to the Andamans on transportation for life. Arrested during October-November 1943. Confined to the Cellular Jail, subjected to torture to confess being British spy. Shot dead on 30 March 1944 at Homfrāygunj in andamans.

Das, Raj Rattan : Born on 1 july 1916, son of Kishen Dass, residence Aberdeen, Port Blair, assistant Jailor. Arrested during

October-November 1943. Shot dead and buried in a mass grave on 30 January 1944 at Homfraygunj, Andamans.

Das, Satyan : Belonged to United Province. Deported to Andamans on transportation for life. Arrested during October – Novemebr 1943 and imprisoned in the Cellular Jail. Shot dead and brried on 30 January 1944 at Homfraygunj by the Japanese Firing Squad.

Das, Bhagwan : Residence Tusnabad village, south Andamans, village Chaudhury, became a member of Indian Independence league. Arrested by the Japanese Force and subjected to inhuman torture in the Cellular Jail. Died in the Cellular Jail on 20 January 1944.

Dhanakdhari, Lall : Son of Lalla Amrit lall, residence Aberdeen, port blair, andamans. Arrested by the Japanese force and tortured in the Cellular Jail. Died on 26 January 1945.

Diwan Singh, Dr. : Born on 12 May 1897, son of Sunder Singh, residence o Galotian Khurd, District Sialkot (now in Pakistan)Took ove the charge of the Cellular Jail Hospital. Came to be known as Dr. Diwan Singh Kalepani. Nominated as President of the Indian Independence League formed at Port blair. Arrested by the Japanese Force under false spy charges in October 1943. Subjected to inhuman torture in the cellular jail. Died on the early hours of 14 January 1944 in wing no. 6 of the Cellular jail.

Dulpan Ram : Residence maharashtra, deported to Andaman Islands. On 30 January 1944 he was shot dead by the Japanese firing Squad at Homfraygunj, Andamans.

David Kaleichnyu : Residence arong village, Tuhet Fang, killed by the Japanese.

David Toopa : Residence Arong Village, Tuhet Kuongpa, killed by the Japanese.

Ebrahim Volimov Kutti : Residence Chukchucha Village, Tuhet Hongsitio, killed by the Japanese.

Esau Isa : Residence Small lapati Village, Tuhet Apung, killed by the Japanese.

Farman Shah : Residence Punjab, deported to Andaman Islands. Joined the Indian Independence League. Arrested by the Japanese Force and incarcerated n the Cellular Jail. Tortured mercilessly in the Jail. Died on 25 January 1944.

Farzand Ali : Born on 5 May 1911, son of Iddo, residence South Point, Port Blair. Arrested during October-November 1943 and kept in the Cellular Jail. Tortured to confess being British spy by the Japanese Imperial Force. Shot dead and buried on 30 January 1944 at Homfraygunj.

Francis Haleh : Residence Arong Village, tuhet Kuongpa, killed by the Japanese.

Francis Poich : Residence small Lapati village, tuhet apung, killed by the Japanese.

Frank William : Residence mus village, Hongehevhaka, an employee of Tanam Hinengo Primary society, killed by the Japanese.

Fulngo : Residence chukchucha Village, Tuhet Pitko, killed by the Japanese.

Gajjan Singh : Residence, Namunaghar, south andamans. Joined the Indian Independence League. Arrested by the Japanese Imperial Force. Shot dead and buried at Homfraygunj on 30 January 1944.

Gopal Krishna, V. : born oon 2 November 1901., son of Pandit Venkat Giri, residence of Aberdeen bazaar, Andamans. Arrested on 22 January 1943 by the Japanese force, subjected to inhuman torture. Shot dead on 30 March 1943 at Dugnabad, Andamans.

Gopal Singh : Residence Namunaghar village, south Andamans, compounder, joined the Indian independence League. Arrested along with his brothers Gajjan singh and

Duleep singh. Shot dead and buried on 30 January 1944 at Homfraygunj, andamans.

Gulab Khan : Residence Bambooflat, south Andamans, employed as a school teacher. Became a member of Indian Independence League, arrested on 1 Novemebr 1943 and incarcerated in the Cellular Jail. Tortured mercilessly to confess being British spy. Died on 21 January 1944 in the Cellular Jail.

Gulam Sarvar : A sepoy of the Indian military force in andamans. Arrested and iimprisoned in the Cellular Jail, tortured shot dead and buried at Homfraygunj on 30 January 1944.

Gyan Singh : Residence homfraygunj village, andamns, became a contractor, joined a the league and liberally donated for its cause, arrested and confined in the Cellular Jail. Shot dead abnd buried at homfraygunj on 30 January 1944.

Hari Kishen : Born on 14 septemeber 1921, son of Ram Charan alias Gappu, residence Junglighat, Port Blair, worked in Jail and Forest Department. Joined the Indian Independence League, arrested and imprisoned in the Jail with his brother Radha krishen. Died on 15 January 1944 due to prolonged torture and absence of medical care.

Harnam Singh : Residence Dundas Point village in south andamans, compounder in the medical department. Became a member of the Indian Independence League, arrested by the Japanese force, confined in the Cellular Jail, taken out to Homfraygunj on 30 january 1944 where h ws shot dead and buried along with other 43 members of the League.

Hussain, Faizal : Belonged to Rawalpindi, sepoy Lance Nail no. 3774 of the Indian Military police, transferred to andamans, joined the League , arrested and imprisoned in the Cellular jail during 1943. On 19 November 1943 he was released from the Jail after being administered with poisonous injection. Died at his residence in Junglighat, Port Blair.

Hachetngo : Residence Malacca Village, tuhet Kameunku, killed by the Japanese.

Haminro Ro Re : Residence Malacca village, tuhet Mingomga murdered by the Japanese.

Hassan Moosa : Residence Chukchucha Village, Tuhet R-ang-tima, killed by the Japanese.

Hussain Mohammed : Residence Chukchucha village, Tuhet Hongsitio, killed by the Japanese.

Jaswant Singh : Born in 1908, son of Chattar Pal, belonged to Bhantu community, settled in Ferrargunj village in south Andamans. Joined the League, arrested during 1943, interned in the Cellular Jail. Shot dead and buried on 30 January 1944 at Homfraygunj.

Jommy Poet Haya : Residence Kenyuaka village, tuhet Kukun, killed by the Japanese soldiers.

John Dawood : Alias naya Pesa, Residence Mus village, tuhet elkupoi, murdered by the Japanese soldiers.

John George : Residence Mus village, Tuhet Apara, murdered by the Japanese soldiers.

Johnson Voo : Residence Arong, tuhet Monti, killed by the Japanese.

Jones(Dr.) : Doctor of Car Nicobar during 1942-45, arrested and killed by the Japanese soldiers.

Karnail Singh : Residence Dundas Point village, south andamans, became a member of the Indian Independence League. Arrested and confined in the Cellular Jail. Shot dead and buried on 30 January 1944 at Homfraygunj.

Kamakin Otnyarah : Residence Arong, tuhet hongcha, killed by the Japanese soldiers at Tomamana Arong.

Kapahih : Residence Perka Village, tuhet totsuruno, murdered by the Japanese at Sokseh, Malacca.

Kas : Residence Tomaloo,Tuhet Hong Tariknyore, killed by the Japanese.

Kaungo : Residence Malaca village, tuhet Re-ang ihong, killed by the Japanese.

Kavoosa : Residence Arong village, tuhet Hong asel, murdered by the Japanese.

Ke-Eya : Residence Malacca village, tuhet hohtomsok, murdered by the Japanese.

Kora : Residence Perka village, tuhet honghora, murdered by the Japanese at Sokseh, Malacca.

Kripiso : Residence perka village, tuhet Honghora, murdered by the Japanese at sokeseh, Malacca during 1942-45.

Lall Singh : Residence Phoenix Bay. Joined the league branch at Port Blair. Arrested and confined in the Cellular Jail.Breathed his last on 23 January 1944 in the cellular Jail due to prolonged torture and absence of proper medicine and food.

Liddar, Sher Singh, Dr. : Born on 13 August 1897 in Punjab. Joined the Indian Independence League during April 1942 and elected as an Executive member. Arrested on 27 October 1943 and confined in the Cellular Jail. Subjected to inhuman torture. Shot dead on 30 January 1944.

Lamuel Lengo : Residence Big Lapati village, tuhet Korovana, killed by the Japanese.

Langara Hachengo : Residence Malacca Village, tuhet Kameunku, murdered by the Japanese.

Mohima Singh : residence dundas point village. Joined the league and actively participated in its meetings. Arrested during October-November 1943, confined in the Cellular Jail, subjected to inhuman torture. Shot dead and buried on 30 January 1944 at Homfraygunj.

Malik, Noor Hussain : Residence North Bay, andamans. Joined Police force during Japanese regime.Arrested in the first week oof January 1944. Shot dead and buried at Homfraygunj on 30 January 1944.

Malkhan Singh : Son of Ganga Ram, belonged to Bhantu community. Arrested and imprisoned in the Cellular Jail, shot dead and buried on 30 January 1944 at Homfraygunj.

Mir Alam : Son of Rehmatullah, born in 1900, employed as Musnshi in Medical Department. Arrested by the Japanese Force, confined in the Cellular Jail, shot dead and buried at Homfraygunj on 30 January 1944.

Mohammed Khan : Residence Haddo, Port Blair. He was arrested and confined in the sixth wing o the Cellular Jail. Taken away to Homfraygunj on 30 January 1944 where he was shot dead and buried.

Mohar Singh : Born on 13 september 1914 in Punjab, son of Murlimal, started business alongwith his brother Jawala singh and Ram singh at Aberdeen Bazaar, Port Blair.Arrested on 12 January 1944 and imprisoned in the Cellular Jail. Subjected to inhuman torture. Shot dead and buried at homfraygunj n 30 January 1944.

Moti Ram : Born on 16 November 1895, son of Babu Ram, Residence Aberdeen village, port blair, high school Teacher. Arrested and confined in the Cellular Jail. Released on 19 November 1943. Died within an hour after release.

Mulkhi Raj : Residence Aberdeen, Port Blair, joined the League. During the mass arrest of the members of the League , he was also arrested and confined in the Cellular Jail. Shot dead and buried at Homfraygunj on 30 January 1944.

Mohammed Ali : Residence Mus village, tuhet Uiyah, murdered by the Japanese at Ku-Inrech, Kinmai village, Car Nicobar.

Mehmood : Residence Chukchucha village, tuhet Hongsitio, killed by the Japanese.

Mathew Kohun : Residence Mus village, tuhet Hoi, an employee of Mus Hostpital murdered by the Japanese.

Milong : Rresidence Arong village, tuhet Hong asel, killed buy the Japanese.

Moses Hayeutu : Residence Arong village, tuhet porovin, killed by the Japanese.

Nag, Pratap Nath : Born on 11 March 1915, son of Ram Naṭh Nag, residence Aberdeen, Port Blair. Arrested during October-Novemebr 1943 and incarcerated in the Cellular Jail. Tortured to confess being British spy. Shot dead and buried on 30 january 1944 at Homfraygunj.

Nag, Surendra Nath (Dr.) : Born on 23 May 1917, son of Ram Nath Nag residence South Point Port Blair. Arrested on 22 January 1943. Shot dead at Dugnabad on 30 March 1943.

Naidu , Muthu Swamy V. : Son of Venkatachallam, born in 1887 in Ross Island, residence south Point, Port Blair. Arrested on 22 January 1943 in the first spy case and incarcerated in the Cellular Jail. Died on 26 January 1943 due to prolonged torture in the Cellular Jail.

Nawab Ali, Khan Saheb : Born on 1 July 1884, son of Wazir ali,residence Aberdeen Bazaar, Port Blair. Played an important role in the formation of Indian Indepnednece League Branch at Port Blair. He was arrested during October-November 1943 and oimprisoned in the Cellular Jail. Due to prolonged torture in the confinement he breathed his last in July 1945.

Niranjan Lal : Born on 15 August 1916, son of Madhusudhan, residence school line, port blair. Joined the League and arrested in September 1944 and incarcerated in the Cellular Jail. Breathed his last on 28 November 1944 in the Cellular Jail.

Noor Ahmed : Residence Phoenix Bay, Port Blair. Shot dead and buried buy Japanese firing squad on 30 January 1944 at Homfraygunj.

Noor Mahi : Residence Phoenix Bay, Port Blair. Worked actively for arousing anti-British feeling. Arrested during October- Novemebr 1943, confined in the Cellular Jail. Shot dead and buried at homfraygunj on 30 January 1944.

Ngaichyem : Residence Arong village, Tuhet Hongkumruh, killed by the Japanese.

Nicoles Siling : Residence Arong Village, Tuhet Otlaraung, killed by the Japanese at Elmanam, Malacca.

Osman : Residence Sawai village, tuhet kaval, murdered by the Japanese.

Otong : Residence Malacca Village, Tuhet Taichsa, murdered by the Japanese.

Pandey, Prem Shankar : Born on 10 May1908, son of Pt. daya shankar Pandey, residence Aberdeen, Port Blair, Sanitary Inspector in the Medical Department, member of many local social organization. Arrrested on 27 October 1943 and confined in the Cellular Jail. Shot dead and buried at Homfraygunj on 30 January 1944.

Paras Ram : Residence Reffargunj village, south andamans, Bhantu. Arrested and tortured to confess being British spy. Shot dead and buried at Homfraygunj on 30 January 1944.

Patti Ram : Born in 1916, son of Mohan, Bhantu, residence Caddlegunj village, south andamans. Joined the League, arrested and incarcerated in the Cellular Jail. Breathed his last on 22 January 1944 in the Cellular Jail.

Paul Lamuel : Residence Big Lapati village, tuhet Korovana, son-in-law of Late Bishop John Richardson, solar system mechanic at the office of Assistant Commissioner, murdered by the Japanese.

Peace : Residence Arong, tuhet Uiti, killed by the Japanese.

Peter Thompson : Residence Mus village, tuhet HJongti Lop, murdered by the Japanese soldiers during their occupation of these Islands.

Poncho : Residence tapoiming village, tuhet Kotopon, murdered by the Japanese soldirers.

Porti Boy : Residence Malacca village , tuhet re- and ihong, murdered by the Japanese.

Poyti : Residence Perka village, tuhet chong, murdered by the Japanese at tamana arong.

Radha Kishen : Born on 15 Septemebr 1911, son of Ram Kishen, residence Junglighat, Head gunner in the forest Department. Joined the league in May 1942. Arrested and incarcerated in the Cellular Jail and subjected to inhuman torture. Shot dead and buried at homfraygunj on 30 January 1944.

Rahalkar, H.H. : Born on 18 July 1909, son of Hari Babu, Engineer at wimco Factory. Arrested by the Japanese Force and imprisoned in the Cellular jail shot dead abnd buried at Homfraygunj on 30 January 1944.

Rao Narayan : Born on 18 January 1914, son of appanna, residence south point, Port Blair. Arrested on 22 January 1943 and interned in the Jail. Subjected to inhuman and barbaric torture. Shot dead on 30 March 1943 at Dugnabad.

Ratan Chand : Born on 8 February 1915, son of Roop Chand, residence Junglighat, employed as a clerk in the Settlement Office,sportsman.Subjected to inhuman tortures by the Japanese force. Shot dead and buried at Homfraygunj on 30 January 1944.

Rahila : Residence chukchucha village, Tuhet Hongsitio, killed by the Japanese.

Rameula : Residence Arong Village, tuhet Uiti, killed by the Japanese at Tomanan Arong.

Ramie : Residence small Lapati village, tuhet Rongi, murdered by the Japanese soldiers.

Rap : Residence arong Village, Tuhet Peteni, murdered by the Japanese.

Richardson, V.A. : Residence Nus village, tuhet apara, son of late John Bishop Richardson, Typist in the Ofiice of asstt. Commissioner, killed by the Japanese.

Roiny : Residence Tamaloo, tuhet hong tariknyore, killed by the Japanese during their occupation of these Islands.

Sahib Singh : Born in 1916, son of Lall singh, Hockey player, elected as an executive member of he League during April 1942. Collected and donated a huge sum of amount to Netaji during his visit to Port Blair. Arrested on 12 january 1944 and interned in the jail. Subjected to inhuman tortures. Shot dead and buried at homfraygunj.

Sangra Singh : Residence Ferrargunj, school Teacher. Joined the league during May 1942 and actively particiapated in it. Arrested and imprisoned in the Cellular Jail. Died on 17 Januyary 1944 in the Cellular Jail due to prolonged torture and confinement.

Sankwa, Lachman Dass : Born on 28 December 1905, son of Chintamani Sankwa, residence Port Blair, employed as a Clerk, later promoted to the post o Tahsildar. Joined the League during April 1942 and was elected as its Secretary. Arrested on 27 Otober 1943 and interned in the Cellular Jail. Shot dead and buried at homfraygunj on 30 January 1944.

Santa Singh : Residence Wimberlygunj, South andamans. Joined the League and arrested in Nevember 1943. Subjected to inhuman tortures. Died on 24 january 1944 iin the Cellular jail as a result o barbaric tortures.

Singhara Singh : Residence phoenix Bay, employed as receiver in the supply department. Breathed his last on 25 January 1944 in the Cellular Jail due to prolonged tortue and confinement.

Suuba Khan, sub-Major : Born on 1 July 1896, sepoy of the Indian Military Police. Arrested on 22 January 1943 and subjected to inhuman torture in the cellular Jail. Shot dead on 30 March 1943 at Dugnabad shore.

Sako, A.S. : Residence Perka village, tuhet sokko, murdered by the japnese at sokseh, Malacca.

Samacha : Residence Arong Village, tuhet Chong, murdered by the Japanese at Tamamana arong.

Samuel Thompson : Residence Mus village, tuhet Hongtilop, killed by the Japanese.

Silki : Residence Arong, Tuhet Hongkumruh, mudered during 1942-45.

Sola : Residence Kenyuaka village, Tuhet Tokumriong, killed by the Japanese, during 1942-45.

Soleman : Residence Sawal village, Tuhet Kaval, murdered by the Japnese at Tomamana Arong.

Solomon Laich : Residence Kakana village, tuhet Hecho, alias la-Eung, businessman, murdered by the Japanese.

Tiwari, Jairam : Son of T. Siroi Ram, residence Aberdeen Bazaar. Joined the League and elected as an Executive member. Donatedliberally for the activities of the League. Arrested on 12 January 1944 and interned in the Cellular Jail. Shot ded and buried at Homfraygunj on 30 January 1944.

Takanya : Residence Perka Village, tuhet otmauk to-oing, murdered by the Japanese at sokseh, Malacca.

Timothy Tavasa : Residence small Lapati village, tuhet Ehten, Catechize in the Church, killed by the Japanese.

Timothy Usku : Residence Mus village, tuhet singi, teacher of missionary school at Car-Nicobar, killed by the Japanese.

Ten : Residence Arong village, Tuhet Hong asel, murdered by Japanese.

Toharuko : Residence Kakana village, tuhet porovin, killed by the Japanese at Ku-inrech at Kinmai.

Tololi : Residence Arong Village, Tuhet porovin, killed by the Japanese at Tomanan Arong.

Topaunyo : Residence Arong Village, Tuhet Alaramlo, thrown into the sea by the Japanese.

Tosa-Olo : Residence Tamaloo Village, tuhet pocho, murdered by the Japanese.

Toyyahamf : Residence Big Lapati village, Tuhet Tumheng, murdered by the Japanese.

Uttam Singh : Residence Phoenix Bay, Port Blair. Joined the League in June 1942 as a Member and actively participated in its affairs. Arrested and confined in the Cellular Jail. Shot dead and buried at Homfraygunj on 30 January 1944.

Umar : Residence Chukchucha village, Tuhet Hongsitio, killed by the Japanese.

Vi-Ingre : Residence Arong village, Tuhet Hongehamoka, murdered by the Japanese at Tomanan Arong.

Yemhong : Residence Kenyuaka village, tuhet Hengkum, killed by the Japanese.

Yeyen : Residence Malacca village, Tuhet Re-ang ihong. Murdered by the Japanese.

Yo-Yo : Residence Malacca Village, tuhet Cochin, murdered by the Japanese.

These details are permanent assets for me. Whenever I get an opportunity or wherever I go, I never forget to get this details mentioned. I may not favour to any body. This is my humble tribute to those unsung heroes who made a history for themselves and will remain immortal in the annals of history till the civilization exists.

During my discussion about this untouched aspects of Andaman with Dr. Panchanand Mishra an eminent Professor of History, he suggested me to incorportate these aspects whenever I plan to write a book on Andaman. Though I heard a lot but I was not getting sufficient materials to move forward in this direction. It was the personal endeavor of Grewal which turned my dream into a reality.

6

Lest We Forget

The end of 2007 added a new chapter in my life. I had to visit a state and a place which I never visualized. Covering a distance of around 1500 KM, I landed at the state capital of Port Blair which though is the part of India, many a ways it is not only different, it gives a look of mini India down in the south and floating in the Bay of Bengal. Mystery still surrounds about the majority of the islands which are vergin and unplundered till date. It is pious the man to be friendly with nature but I have noticed the other side of the picture too. During my stay there I was told that a number of people preferred to commit suicide when they did not find way to leave the islands. I do not know as to what extent this was a story or a myth but I reached to a conclusion that if an outsider being posted there is not allowed to visit the main land during frequent intervals, his bent of mind will be towards the negative direction. Reasons are obvious. One finds himself in different type of situation compared to the main land. Loneliness and solitude may be blessings for a group of people, it may effect adversely also.

My first meeting with Grewal compelled me to ask – "you belong to this place or a settler"?

I belong to this place though my father was a settler. This was his befiting reply. He told me that long back in 1969 his father Shri Amarjit Singh Grewal came to Port Blair along with his Grand Father. He was serving in Border Security Force and during the regime of Mrs. Gandhi the Ex-servicemen were sent to Andaman. The govt. had given each of them around 15 acres of land for their survival. Around 72 families sail to Port Blair from Kolkata and reached there, by ship. The journey took five days. They were again transported to Camp Bell Bay by T.S.Jarwa the only ship available during those days. This journey took around four days. During those days there were no port or harbours available in between Port Blair and Sadar Group of islands. The passengers were advised for not leaving the ship till the same was finally anchored anchored at the last destination of Camp Bell Way. These settlers were provided food and basic amenities by the Govt. Grewal also told me that the Govt. officers used to allure the visitors with land and post, so that they might prefer to settle in the islands. I have the occasion to take around these islands with Grewal within a short span of two years. It was a privilege to meet a few settlers along with his parents who were unfortunately living in Govt. shelters after the destruction of their life and property by the Tsunami in 2004. They were reduced to same position what they had faced at the time of landing at Great Nicobar. This did not deter their ideas. During my formal chat with Shri Amarjit Singh he vehemently denied for having any ideas in my for leaving these islands at the time of distress.

"We came here long back. This is my third generation. We laboured and survive. My children studied and doing their job. What I have to do in Punjab now? This is my homeland." This can be the utterances of a greatman only who was ready to face the eventualities of life without being an escapist.

I remember my sailing with Grewal to Camp Bell Bay by M.V.Kalighat from Port Blair. The ship takes around 40 hours to reach Camp Bell Bay via Noncowery, a nature made harbour. Throughout the journey Grewal made me acquainted with the different islands falling in between after the over night journey, the ship ancquerred at Noncowvery for about two hours then sailed for Camp Bell Bay. These ships are the life line of the Andaman and Nicobar group of islands and cattering the need of the local people besides transportation from one place to another. Despite the availability of modern amenities in these islands, even today you cannot plan your journey if you have to travel from one islands to another which is not connected by road. I could try to understand the feelings of the local residence of Camp Bell Bay whenever I visited there. One day, during lunch, when I asked one of the relatives of Grewal as to what was his feelings about these islands especially after Tsunami. He came with a bold face and his reply was "Tsunami came and went away. That was an unfortunate event. We now do not remember those days and we do not even planning to leave these islands. Govt. has provided all the facilities. We have a very good hospital equipped with Doctors and medicines, administrative as well as judicial set up and police for the protection. The only thing is that we cannot plan our journey. It all depends on the sailing of the ship, helicopter service as well the mood of climate and the sky."

Mr. Viraya used to be the Dy. Director of Shipping those days he had told me how the sailing of the ships are planned especially in the months end in order to ensure the payment of the survey of the public servants working there. These ships start from Port Blair twice or thrice in the month and goes to Campbell Bay via Car Nicobar, Nancowry Kachhal and Chaura. These ships can be said to the life line of the people living in the southern group of the islands. These small islands are well looked after by the administration. Atleast, one Police post and a few civil functionaries are representing the administration each of the islands inhabited by the people. The life is very hard in these islands and one day when I insisted to visit Nicobar by the only ship available T.S. Jarwa, I was discouraged by Grewal because of the rough weather. "It is better to avoid the journey during rains". He told.

Why, when others are going, why not we?

After a few minutes Viraya rang me up with the same request. Probably Grewal had told about insistence.

"But I want to take this adventure." Viraya laughed but did not discourage me further.

At the Haddo Warf, I was told at the sailing of the ships was cancelled due to the rough weather and M.V. Kalighat would be sailing up to Hutbay only.

Grewal appeared to be satisfied with these developments. Immediately he gave a ring to swamy for the vehicle. "I had told you Sir, one should not venture to go to the sea during rough weather. It is very risky."

"Are you seeing the crowd?" Can you imgine their plight? What they would do now? Thereafter I was told the hardships the islanders face. Their movements to the other islands can not be planned. It as such materializes as for the mood of the sea. The people going to Car Nicobar "would have to wait till the announcement of next schedule." Grewal told me.

What was the reason of cancellation of the Journey?

Ships are helpless in the high sea. They struggle to sail."

Grewal had definitely told me to discourage but I was also firm in my idea.

Please don't call Swamy. Let us go and enjoy the journey of Hutbay.

He took around 8 hours to sail up to Hutbay against the normal jouney of 4 hours by M.V. Kalighat. The speed boats are covering the jouney in 6 hours. The ship was definitely struggling to survive in the open sea. We planned to say at Hutbay for two days. It's a beautiful small island in the radious of 22 Kms. The small township is dominated by Bengali population. All govt.

offices are functional here including the state transport department. The area is very beautiful as well as peaceful. Being a flight island and in the open sea the coastal area was badly damaged during Tsunami. The govt. had now made a rehabilitation centre at the top of the hill and it's a marvel of modern architecture.

I got the opportunity of visiting Hut Bay on a number of occasions. In fact, it was one of the places I liked much. In Port Blair people survive on rain harvesting technology. In Hut Bay there is plenty of water and inside the jungle beautiful stream, water falling from the top of the hill. It is a beautiful place. Just imagine of a stream of sweet watch in a small island which is surrounded by high sea. Only mother nature can deliver this type of beauty. In this small town-ship everything is available. The most memorable visit was on 25th of January 2009 when the public sentiments on the Republic Day was worth to be noticed. Celebration, like this on an island located at a distance of 1500 Kms from the mainland make us proud and we feel – he this part fo the land is also ours - belonging to the govt. of India. The 'Prabhat Pheri', national songs and cultural activities in schools and govt. departments left an everlasting imprint on my mind. The Govt. house of Andaman Public Works Department is a nice place to stay in Hut Bay. The local market given an impression that you are in a small principality of West Bengal. This place however, lacks higher education and expert medical facilities are is holely and solely dependent on Port Blair. The speed boat to going daily to Hut Bay from Port Blair and one big ship 'M.V. Deril' is also pressed into service.

Twice I had the occasion to visit Car Nicobar, the District Head Quarter of Sout Andaman, a city badly devastated by Tsunami and reportedly half of the population was sweped away by the mighty waves which invaded the city from all the four sides. This is the restricted area and only Govt. Servants are allowed to visit from the Port Blair there is a regular service of

Helicopter from Port Blair once daily whereas the schedule of the ship is decided on weekly basis or sometimes twice in a week. It takes around 12 hours to reach Car Nicobar from Haddo Warraf of Port Blair. By helicopter it can be reached in one and a half hour. There is nothing worth seeing and the city is consigned in less than half kilometer and in a circle. The govt. offices, hospitals as well as the shops everything are confined. It is dominated by the Nicobaris – a tribe which is now in mainstream and educated in comparison to others. The only place of stay is the Andaman PWD Guest House. I was told during Tsunami, the single story guest house was almost summerged when the level of the water was at part with the roof of the guest house. Fortunately the volume of the water reduced and life could be saved at the cost of heavy damage of the property. These southern group of islands are different from the townships of Mayabandar and Diglipur. Development can be noticed there because of their connectivity by both road and sea. The small townships of Mayabandar and Diglipur were just like Ganga and the only road of this area i.e. ATR terminates at Diglipur. The beautiful guest house of Mayabandar is the only place of attraction otherwise there is nothing worth memorable in this petty island although it is the District Head Quarter of middle Andaman.

During my stay at Port Blair, I came into contact with a number of persons who were born and bought up in Andaman and now holding key post in the various department of the Administration as well as in Health Directorate. Just imagine the hardship they might have faced when the means of communications were not developed and people were at the mercy of the natural calamities in the islands. Still, they fought for survival, pursued their studies, participated in the freedom struggle and left an example that hard work and perseverance are appreciated in the world. Obviously, they never leaved and are not leaving under any concept which was named and designed as Kalapani during the British rule. This place is full of tales of bravery, enthusiasm and lust for life against the hardships of nature. There is not even a sense of demoralization I could find among the local people who have built up and contributed to the development of these beautiful islands which are now the integral part of the country.

I remember what Shri P.K. Subash told me Director, Doordarshan, Port Blair. "This is a beautiful place to work without tension or interference. The land is very fertile for research oriented or carrying out the programmes of the govt. and the implementation of various projects. Only thing is that you try and prefer to live with your family or else you will feel alone which might lead to depression." I personally felt that Subash was not biased. He had worked a lot in this islands and before his departure he also ensured visiting all the important islands. Once he had told me that he had got the orders of transfer and he would always feel not visiting Campbell Bay. Surprisingly, one day when I asked the Doctor his location, he told me that on the request of Subash he had accompanied him and they were staying at the PWD Guest House of the Campbell Way.

I also must mention about the beautiful resort located at the top of Port Blair named as Megaport resort. It is a hotel with Restaurant and Bar run by Andaman Administration. It is a nice place to stay and chatt with personal friends in the open restaurant at the lap of the nature.

I knew my departure from Port Blair was imminent and sonner or later I would be landing in the mainland. Believe me, I have not forgotten the islands and the beautiful people whom I met and interacted. Shri S.S. Grewal and Swamy were my two eyes whereas he was doctor who remain with me all the times even at the cost of his personal work and still he has not made any distance from me. Subash is now posted at Director, Doordarshan, Port Blair and we are in touch. C.Udaikumar was holding some of the powerful posts in the administration and he always stood by me at the time of need and crisis. My domestic help Prasad still remembers me and I never forget to take account of his personal problems whenever I get the opportunity. Navin Jha and Manoj Kumar Jha were my neighbours and they are still there ar still in Port Blair. The civil engineers namely Pushpraj, Dutta Babu as he was popularly known and Mr. Subramaniam are still there and during my visit they welcomed me in full spirit. I am yet to see a gentleman like K.Moiuddin, working in local administration and full of emotions and sense of hospitality.

Whenever I feel of human sentiments, I found Andaman, dominating the main lander. There are sense of hospitality, simple style of living, are of enteracting with the people are far ahead in comparison to the people of mainland who decided everything by and large in their own interest and not emotionally and with a sense of sentiment.

There is nothing like Kalapani which I could found in the islands. Beauty never fades if you throw mud on the nature. It will come out with freshness. The Britishers had done this to hide their ugly face of terrorism and sadism on the pretext of development and democracy but they could not continue and were badly exposed before they left this country.

I must confess that there are still few officers who allow the human sentiments to prevail and they do not let down the subordinates morally even in the days of crisis and the things became out of control and they also become helpless for the time being. Due to some compelling reasons, I had to remain alone in Port Blair and my problems were obvious. Frequent visit to look after the family in the main land was too expensive to bear. My immediate superior Shri D. Kashyap IPS took care of me and my family in the mainland despite his own ill health till I came back to join my family. My other collegues Mr Mansukh, Diptendu, Sumit, Alok and Arup were always with me during my posting in Andaman. My successor.

Sh. A.K. Banerjee ultimately become instrumented for my

safe departure from Andaman for a new posting. I should acknowledge here the version of Mrs. Rushida Iqbal, Curator National Memorial collector Jail, Portblair for giving many informations about Mortyrs imprisoned in cellular jail and even she informed that many papers, documents and archival materials were carried away by the Britishers, otherwise, we could have traced more details of freedom fighters imprisoned here. I have the privilege and fortune to work under great human beings likes Shree Ranjit Sinha IPS and Director General of Police, J. Ahmed IPS, Vijay Kumar Singh IPS and D.K. Thakur IPS who not only possess highest degree of professional competence, but I always noticed their dedication towards the human value and never found them compromising with that. These are the rarest qualities which makes the persons distinguished. I just recall the words of Ravindra Nath Tagore "Every child who is born is an indication that God has not lost hope in mankind." The kind of love and affection I got from them encouraged me to face the crisis of life and the cloud of uncertainty.

7

The Tale of Tsunami

"But what of life whose bitter hungry sea
Flows at our heels, and gloom of sunless night
Covers the day which never more return ?
Ambition, love and all the thoughts that burn
We lose too soon, and only find delight
In withered husks of some dead memory"

From: "Dsespoir" (Oscar Wilde)

The dawn of 21st Century brought bad news for Andaman & Nicobar Island. The beauty of the Islands was eclipsed with the devastating Tsunami which not only shook the islands for few seconds, brought devastation and miseries which was unparallel in the contemporary history. It was the worst attack of the Mother Nature on both life and property and what my predecessor, a victim and eye witness told me "the land was trembling, tramours were unbearable followed by heavy rainful. It took two minutes from coming down from the third floor of the govt. building and we used to loose balance after two or three steps before we could touch the ground. There was a complete black out. People were in panic and in a fix. Children were crying. Rumour was coming that the sea water had entered the city with full force, big cracks were noticed throughout the city and everything is likely to be submerged within a few minutes."

On the first opportunity many including my predecessor had shifted their family to the mainland and preferred to live along in the islands.

Another eyewitness had told me that he along with many others had rushed to the water sports complex Port Blair. When the news spread that sea water had reduced, had gone back and only sand is visible. All of a sudden, the mightly waves appeared and as I was told that waves almost six meters in height invaded the coast with a draconian speed of around 250 Km per hour. It happened thrice within five minutes and the receding waves caused devastation and added a new chapter in the history. Andaman Nicobar was the worst affected and the population and govt. installations were washed away by the angry waves. Half of Kachhal portion of Campbell bay and Indira point till today exist on paper only.

I could recollect when Grewal was telling me these things with tears in his eyes. In Campbell Bay, I could see the remnant of his house. A small portion of kitchen was the only testimony of the big house which was constructed by his father long back. The octogenerion Sardarji reminciences that period which took away everything from him - what he had earned during his lifetime.

"I saw the violent waves and the rising level of water." Smelling some rat. I shouted for everybody just to vacate their respective premises and to run away to a higher place as early as possible.

"The brave soldiers never give up "– and I saw this jeal in Amarjeet Singh. When I asked "What is your planning now? Are you planning to shift from this island?

"Definitely not. I have seen good days in this island. We created one small world here - My Children were born and brought up in this island. There is no question of going back.

Government has also given full support. Permanent shelters are under construction "– What a bold face? A true soldier is letter and spirit. I was deeply moved by the hospitality of this family and believe me, everytime I talk to Grewal, Our conversation either started or ended with the question – "what about our trip to Campbel Bay upto Indira Point? The magnificient statue of Mrs. Indira Gandhi has been erected at the fartherest end of our Geographical boundary which was badly devastated during Tsunami. The approach road is under construction and expected to be motarable by the end of 2012.

Andaman and Nicobar Islands the silent spectator of the natural calamity- which brought tears for the people – did never complaint. The people bore the burnt but did not escape. The administration and the government delivered their best. It was because of the mutual cooperation and the wonderful work done by the Andaman Public Wroks Department. The islands could be rebuilt and reconstructed. The faith of people has been restored but not the lost property. Acres of fertile land has become sterile due to salty water, coconut plantations have been damaged, beaches have been destroyed and quality fishes like Prawan and lobstars have almost disappeared from the cost.

I was told how the thousands of tourists had to wait in the island on the days of tsunami because of the cancellation of air services as well the ships. People were somehow in deported to the main land by the special flights and they floated bad news and rumours about the islands, not withstanding the facts the local people being conscious of the rights and duties, work to shoulder to shoulder with the administrative functionaries and a matter of fact because of their confidence only the govt. skipped debates on this issue and constructed in the reconstruction of the islands.

The situation was different from mainland and rehabilitation was not that easy. Problems could be visualized because of the location of these islands, far off from the mainland. The islands are dependant on the mainland of India. The ships are virtually the lifeline and cater the entire need of the people. In normal course it sails twice or thrice in the month from the mainland and right from bread and butter to medicine are transported through the ports of Kolkata and Chennai. In normal course it takes around three to four days to reach a ship to Haddo warf of Port Blair. The sailing is thoroughly dependant on the weather and mood of the sea. After a consignment reaches Port Blair, it is further shifted to other small islands. The consignments include foodgrain to heavy machinery/vehicles apart from the raw materials required for construction/ reconstruction. This challenging work was undertaken by the administration and the people now do not look back to those backdays. They face the situation boldly, did not leave their places of stay thereby setting an example of determination, tolerance and perceiverance.

As an abandunt precaution, the administration has put a restriction and the natural resources are not to be touched without the consent of the administration. The jungles and its byproducts, sand and the property of the sea except some varieties of fishes are in the list of prohibited items. The only plywood factory is now closed. The different type of problems is now emerging. The wooden buildings are being replaced by RCC works, which is an extra load on the islands.

2004 Indian Ocean earthquake

The Andaman and Nicobar Islands comprise 572 islands (all land masses in both low and high tides) out of which 38 are inhabited, both by people from the mainland and indigenous tribes. The islands lie just north of the earthquake epicentre, and the tsunami reached a height of 15 m in the southern Nicobar Islands. The official death toll is 812, and about 7,000 are still missing. The unofficial death toll (including those missing and presumed dead) is estimated to be about 7,000.

The Great Nicobar and Car Nicobar islands were the worst hit among all the islands because of their proximity to the quake and relative flatness. Aftershocks continue to rock the area. One fifth of the population of the Nicobar Islands is said to be dead, injured or missing. Chowra Island has lost two thirds of its population of 1,500. Entire islands have been washed away, and the island of Trinket has been split in two. Communications have not been restored with the Nancowry group of islands, some of which have been completely submerged, with the total number of the population still out of contact exceeding 7,000.

Among the casualties in Car Nicobar, 100 Indian Air Force personnel and their family members were washed away when the wave hit their air base, which was reported to have been severely damaged. The St. Thomas Cathedral (also known as the John Richardson church after John Richardson, a missionary and member of parliament) was washed away. The church, established in 1930 was one of the oldest and prominent churches in the region. A cricket stadium named after John Richardson and a statue dedicated to him were also washed away.

The majority of the population of Andaman Islands is made up of people from the mainland, mostly from West Bengal and Tamil Nadu. The natives of Andaman and Nicobar Islands are endangered tribal groups, such as such as the Jarawa, the Sentinelese, the Shompen, the Onge and the Andamanese. They are regarded as anthropologically significant as they are some of the world's most primitive tribes and considered the world's only link to ancient civilisation. Most of these tribes have maintained their aboriginal lifestyle for centuries, and government policy has been to not interfere with them unless absolutely essential.

It is reported that most of the native islanders survived the tsunami because they live on higher ground or far from the coast. The Onge (with a 2001 census population of 96), Jarawa (240), Sentinelese (39) and Andamanese (43) have been reached by survey teams and are confirmed to be safe although the number of dead is unknown. The Sentinelese live on a reserved island and are hostile to outsiders which is making it difficult for Indian officials to visit the island. They have shot arrows at helicopters sent to check on them. In the Nicobar Islands, the Nicobarese, a Mongoloid tribe (2001 population of 28,653), have lost about 656 lives with 3,000 still missing. Surveys are being conducted on the Shompen (2001 census count of 398) located on GreatNicobar is land.

India's only active volcano, Barren 1, located at Barren Island 135 kilometres (80 miles) northeast of the capital Port Blair, erupted because of increased seismic activity on 30 December 2004. People have been evacuated since then and there have been no reports of any casualties.

On December 26 2004, an earthquake with a moment magnitude of 9.3 occurred along Northern, Sumatra and the Nicobar and Andaman Islands that resulted in the catastrophic tsunami that affected 12 countries (figure 1.1). A second earthquake took place on March 28 close to the Island Nias with a moment magnitude of 8.6 1 2. The human impact of the tsunami on December 26 2004 was enormous: more than 175.000 people killed and almost 2 million affected. Many people lost their homes and had to find shelter with family, friends or in temporary settlements. Four countries, Indonesia, Sri Lanka, India and Thailand were worst hit with Indonesia bearing the reatest burden with nearly three-quarters of all dead and over half the omeless. The tsunami also destroyed physical infrastructure such as roads, hospitals, schools and bridges. Essential services such as health care and education broke down due to loss of staff, materials and structures. Communicable disease outbreaks, which have a devastating potential in emergency situations were foreseen in the aftermath of the disaster 4-6. The large number of dead bodies gave rise to widespread fear of diseases and epidemics of malaria, cholera and dengue were expected. Evidence from previous natural disasters however, has shown that disease outbreaks are a very rare Occurrence and it is well established that dead bodies do not pose a health threat.

8

Andaman Today

I was told by Grewal that many survivors are settled in Sadipur area of Port Blair. One Mr. Gauri Shankar Pandey is still alive. He has crossed the age of 90. He is hearing impaired now and losing in memory also. When I contacted him, was not even in a position to talk. He is staying at Dighabad area of Port Blair. His dependeants told me that the Japanese were in the habit of torturing the Indian even on little suspicion and even used to throw them in the open sea. Sri Motilal a resident of Brijganj told that depite odds that period was better than present. Sri Mohanlal of Sadipur is counting his last days. Physically fit Sardar Swarn singh was recently facilitated by the govt. of India.The freedom fighter of Andaman formed an association under the banner of Andaman political prisoners Fraternity circle and Subsequently on their demand, the Cellular Jail was dedicated to the nation by the Late Prime Minister Shri Morarzi Desai and became as national movement.

An unforeseen problem was visualized in respect of thos convicts who underwent the sentences passed by the court. The problem was how to deal with them in the Island which was far off from their native place and deportation was not that easy because of lack of transportation facilities. Coming to mainland was not that easy. The British planned to rehabilitate them in Andaman itself. They even tried to bring their families from the mainland but that too was not easy. Hindus considered it as taboo to cross the sea. Some released prisoners were knotted to matrimonial alliances and by and large the scheme though was not very much successful, it led to the establishment of casteless and classless society.

Andaman today is probably the only place where people of all parts of India could be found but all of them speak Hindi. Hthe concept of casteism is not predominant. The aged people do have the feeling that they belong to mainland, the generation to come will be andamani only in true sense of the term. A peculiar social syntethesis is likely to emerge in new future. Children are going to main land for higher education. Obviously job opportunitiesfor technocrats, doctors and civil servants are not sufficient in this island to accommodate each and everyone who belogs to the Island. This may lead to exodus from these islands since frequent visits at short intervals to these islands is not possible. Apart from being expensive this will remain a nightmare for the people belonging to the southern group of the islands. This will compel the exodus of the literate people who some how fail to get employment in Andaman. The ultimate survivors will be the business class and the illiterate people who would continue to survive on the govt. donated land and engaged in private trade.

Andaman and Nicobar Islands of India are diverse in all respects. The Socio-economic and political set up is entirely different from mainland India. It constitute one of the most important Union Territory and has been described as a Miniature India, and aptly so. Of course there are many problems including migration, unemployment and population increase and scarcity of water and land in these Islands that it need some elaboration, which this study intends to undertaken.

Andaman and Nicobar Islands, formerly known as Kalapani (the dark waters) located in the midst of Bay of Bengal, is a district Union Territory came into existence by the Government of India Act of 1956. The administrative boundary of this Union Territory includes all the islets, stretched over a region of 740 kilometers from north to south with an intervention of about 130 kilometers between Andaman and Nicobar group of islands. In fact, it is largest island territory of India consisting of 572 Islands, islets, rocks in the archipelago, while only about 300 Islands are appreciable size, and they stretch approximately eight hundred kilometers longitudinally in a slightly bow shaped. Of these only 39 Islands has been inhabited so far. Many of the Islands are named after the British Generals who have fought bravely during the Great Revolt of 1857 namely Neil, Havelock, Camp Bell and many more. The northern point of landfall Island, which is 901 kilometers away from the mouth of Hooghly River and about 190 kilometers from Myanmar (Burma). Similarly the southern-most tip of Islands which is known Indira Point (Pygmalion Point) is only about 150 kilometers away from Sumatra (Indonesia). Most of the Islands are unfit for permanent human habitation as they are too small and have no drinking water. Rain pouring 265 days in the year, make the virgin forest, tropical and thickly dense.

Shipping has remained important throughout the plan. Roads and Bridges and Forestry emerged important in the 5th plan. Planning Commission has put up major thrust on Inter-Islands and Island-Mainland shipping service and general education. But up to the Fifth Plan no firm indication was there of the growth promoting export oriented approaches about which we hear so much.

There are about 722 kms of roads in various Islands, of which 506 kms falls in rural areas. The APWD have transferred 182 kms of rural roads in Andamans to the PRIs. Although no separate funds is provided by the Administrative for maintenance of these roads, action has been initiated for repair and maintain the transferred roads from the funds provided under Road Sector.

Works have also been taken up at various places to provide connectivity in the rural areas by constructing new rural roads, bridges, culverts.

In these Islands, there are 172 villages which require augmentation of water supply. The water supply in these villages is not enough as per norms. Water treatment plants are only available at few places like Diglipur, Rangat, Mayabunder, Bakultala, Bamboo flat, and Kamorta etc. However at other places only raw water with chlorination is being supplied. The Zilla Parishad has taken up works at various places to install water treatment plant to ensure supply of safe drinking water. Such plant has been installed at North Wandoor, Havelock, Neil Islands, Desratpur (Rangat) and Tugapur (Mayabunder).

In order to augment water supply in rural areas under PMGY projects in various places would be completed. The National Hydro Power Corportion (NHPC), New Delhi, has been entrusted to take up Krishna Nallah project in Little Andman. A detailed project report amounting 3.27 crores received from NHPC has already been submitted to the Administration for clearance. An amount of Rs. 2.15 Crores has already been deposited with NPHC for the execution of the work. In addition to the above, Zilla Parishad has identified 15 villages under TPP during 2004-2005 which are partially covered. The water supply in these villages will be augmented by constructing ring well and check dams etc., in order to make them fully covered villages as per norms.

In order to provide quality education in the rural areas, the Zilla Parishad is implementing in scheme "Construction of Vivekanada Kendra Zila Parishad Vidyalayas" at various places in the islands. The scheme envisages creation of infrastructure facilities such as land, building and furniture etc, apart from maintenance of the building. The school will be run by the non-governmental organization / institution.

During 9th Five Year Plan an amount of Rs. 5.00 crores was released for the establishment of five schools in rural areas. Schools at Chouldari, Pahalgaon, Basantipur, Kadamtala and Diglipur have been completed up to primary stage and have already started functioning. A Memorandum of Understanding to provide quality education in these schools for pupil of rural areas was signed between the Zila Parishad, Port Blair and Vivekananda Kendra Sangatan, Kanya Kumari.

Apart from the above the Zila Parishad is also planning to construct few more new schools VKZPV at Garacharma, Shore Point (Bamboo flat) and Campbell Bay besides upgrading the existing schools. The estimate for construction of senior school at Diglipur and Chouldari has already been sent to the administration for approval. During the 10th Five Year Plan the administration has so far released Rs. 5 crores for the completion of ongoing works as well as to construct more new schools one each at Burmanalla, Tusnabad, and Baratang and Karma tang.

There are more than 500 villages in the Islands which do not have proper irrigation facilities. It is proposed to construct small check dams/weir/well/pond at various villages. Earthen canal, dyke etc, will also be constructed to improve the ground water source. The Zilla Parishad has also included a programme in the 10th plan to utilize tail end ground water from Kalpong dam for irrigation purpose. Though administrative and financial autonomy has been given to Zilla Parishad to a large extent, but here is need to enhance the powers of PRIs for easy and speedy implementation of various work. The PRIs in the Islands have been striving to provide basic minimum needs to the villagers for enlistment of their living standard especially in road, water, education sector and other public needs for rapid development of the Union Territory.

The December 2004 M 9.0 earthquake and the subsequent tsunami caused immense ecological changes to both island groups, including taking a toll on human life, human life patterns for indigenous groups in the Nicobars, infrastructure, and permanent change to agriculture lands and plantations. The quake and tectonic plate shifts resulted in upheaval of most Andaman Islands including Little Andaman Island, causing upliftment of reef flats, drying of mangrove creeks, drying of mangrove strands and shifting of strands into creeks.

The subsidence of the southern South Andaman Island and the Nicobars have caused major impacts on coastal ecosystems, fauna, flora and freshwater systems, besides most marine turtle nesting beaches have been washed away.

Encroachment remains the major problem affecting the forest cover. Encroachment problem is linked to the increase in the number of families originally settled in the islands due to expansion and also uncontrolled immigration into the islands. Encroachments lead to forest fragmentation, reduction in forest cover, and its conversion to monocultures leading to loss of biodiversity. Encroachments also lead to degradation of the forests near them due to illegal collection of forest resources. Each encroachment pocket became a nucleus for further encroachments and degradation of adjacent forest areas.

Settlers have been allotted hilly lands for horticulture. They were permitted to extract and sell the timber on these lands, on payment of royalty to the government, if the Department of Environment and Forests was unable to clear the area for horticulture. Since they do not have the infrastructure to do this, middle men do it for them. In the process the land is cleared and erosion takes place. Such lands under normal circumstances are to be converted into horticulture, usually for the cultivation of area nut, coconut or spices, but in certain cases they have not been converted so far and are lying fallow and eroded. There are also large tracts of allotted land covered by forest growth. As per the Hon'ble Supreme Court ruling, all such areas come under definition of forest for the purpose of Forest (Conservation) Act, 1980. These areas need to be dealt with accordingly.

Collection of shells and sea cucumbers for commercial purposes has led to a drastic decline in the occurrence of these two taxa. While they are protected now, the Department of Environment and Forests has not been given the additional resources necessary to enforce the ban on their collection. Assessing reef areas has been identified as a research priority during a seminar on protected areas planning. Degradation has been recorded at a few sites. However, the overall condition of the coral resource in the Andamans is poorly documented; only one detailed study has been conducted, in the vicinity of the MGMNP (Kulkarni, 2000). A recent UNDP/ZSI study has identified newer species of coral in the Andamans taking the recorded coral species number from 197 to 235.

However coral reefs of the islands are under various degrees of threat such as siltation, sand mining, agricultural runoff and damage due to fishing and tourism activities. These are apart from global climatic factors such as sea temperature rise. Remedial measures would have to emphasise the control of further encroachment of forestland and its consequent degradation. This is because sedimentation from the land clearing is one of the main causes of coral mortality (Whitaker, 1994; Kulkarni, 2000; 2001).

Tourists stepping on the corals also cause damage. The reefs around the main tourist sites of Jolly Buoy and Redskin Islands, in the MGMNP, have been degraded due to this reason. Remedial measures would include restricting the numbers of tourists visiting the MGMNP, as well as a proper awareness programme to educate them on how to prevent damage to corals (Kulkarni, 2000; Singh et al, 2002). There is no recent information from the RJMNP; this becomes a priority since a number of dive shops and adventure tour operators have sprung up in the last couple of years.

There are four groups of indigenous tribes in the Andamans and two in the Nicobars. Their populations are generally showing declining trends except that of the Nicobarese, who are well assimilated into the mainstream. A comparative table of the populations of various tribes is given in Table 4.

The Great Andamanese are confined to Strait Island. The Onge are under constant disturbance from poachers and settlers in Little Andaman Island. The Sentinelese, still hostile, are undisturbed. However fishermen and lobster divers have been observed very close to coastline and inside bays of this island. This may be keeping the Sentinelese away from foraging in the intertidal reefs during low tide and from fishing out at sea in their dugout canoes (Andrews, per. Observ.)

The fourth tribe, the Jarawa, typify the debate ongoing in the islands. They were hostile until five years ago. Recent shedding of hostility has resulted in frequent contacts with settlers and passengers along the Andaman Trunk Road (ATR). The administration is taking action to reduce the contacts.

One school of thought believes that it is necessary to enable the Jarawa to abandon their forest existence and bring the benefits of "civilization" to them. Opposed to this is the vies that they should be left strictly alone; otherwise they will become extinct. Supporting the latter view are the case histories of what happened to the Andamanese and the Onge tribes (Portman, 1899).

The Government of India has recently finalized its policy on the Jarawas. The objectives of the policy are (i) to protect the Jarawas from the harmful effects of exposure and contact with the outside world while they are not physically, socially and culturally prepared for such an interface, (ii) to preserve the social organization, mode of subsistence and cultural identity of the Jarawa community, (iii) to provide medical help to the Jarawas to reduce mortality and morbidity in case of their sudden affliction with diseases, which their systems are unaccustomed to; (iv) to conserve the ecology and environment of the Jarawa Reserve Territory and strengthen the support systems in order to enable the Jarawas pursue their traditional modes of subsistence and way of life, and (v) to sensitise the settler communities around the Jarawa habitat and personnel working for the protection and preservation of the Jarawas about the need to preserve this ancient community and to value their unique culture and lifestyle. With the said objectives in view, the Government of India has framed various strategies and guidelines for the protection and welfare of the Jarawas. The strategies include (a) protection of cultural identity by a policy of maximum autonomy to Jarawas with minimum and regulated intervention by the Government, (b) protectionof the natural habitat with no exploitation of natural resources within the tribal reserve and a ban on interaction between tourists and the Jarawas, (c) protection of health status by a periodic health surveys and extension of medical assistance in the Jarawa area itself, (d) regulation of traffic on the ATR by limiting it to the essential purposes of public transport, supplies and emergency evacuation of patients with movement only during restricted hours and in convoys, (e) Codification of the Jarawa language, so that the officials of the Administration, who are required to come in contact with the Jarawas, are able to communicate with them and understand their perception, reactions and problems, and (f) suitable institutional arrangements for the protection and welfare of all the aboriginal tribes including the Jarawas.

The recent order of the Supreme Court is to close the ATR in the section passing through the Jarawa Triabal Reserve, but the A & N Administration has approached the Court for modification of the Order.

Also at stake here are the largest relatively undisturbed tracts of forests within the islands: the Jarawa Reserve, the Onge Reserve on Little Andaman Islands, and the Great Nicobar Biosphere Reserve, which acts as a home to the majority of the Shompen. Assimilation of the tribes into the mainstream is likely to increase pressure on the lands within the reserve for logging and encroachment, as well as increase in poaching activies.

Developmental activities involving RCC structures require large quantities of sand. This sand is quarried from the beaches. While the Forest department gets royalty on the sand mined, and the sand taken from each area is regulated, this is difficult to enforce in practice. As a result, erosion of beaches has occurred. This has had three major consequences: loss of land and coastal forests, the loss of 21 sea turtle nesting beaches in ANI, and the loss of recreational areas (Andrews, et al., 2001).

In its order, the Supreme Court has ordered that the amount of sand utilized must be reduced to 33% of its current usage within five years. The current system of monitoring needs to be strengthened to enforce this.

The Port Management Board constructs jetties on remote islands. These jetties very often block the free flow of sand across the beaches. This results in a pile up of sand on one side of the jetty and erosion of sand on the other side. Computer models exist now to predict the erosion that might occur and to design appropriate structures. These are required to be used while designing jetties and deciding on their location.

Tourism development in the islands in the last decade, has led to the unplanned development of several areas. The numbers of tourists are increasing in spite of the lack of sufficient facilities. This has led to pollution using plastic (controlled only in the MGMNP), camping on sea turtle beaches and preventing their nesting, for example, on Ross and Smith Islands and on Little Andaman Island (Andrews, et al., 2001). Forest fires starter by camping tourists have also occurred at Chidiatapu, New Wandoor and on Havelock Islands. Forest fires especially in coastal forests, cultural contamination resulting from esposure to drugs and nudity, and loss to the exchequer due to tourists benefiting from the subsidies on transport, are likely hazards of promoting uncontrolled tourism. Construction of hotels at several locations to accommodate the tourists will result in problems such as garbage removal, effluent release and habitat degradation.

The 2001 census reports a population of 3.57 lakhs. Significant increase in the population is due to immigration from the mainland States. The control of immigration becomes one of the top priorities if biodiversity is to be conserved in these islands. The introduction of an island identity card and inner line permit is a first step in this direction, besides elimination of the subsidy on passenger fares for ships.

This department licences fishing boats and fishing/shell fishing in earmarked areas, maintains fisheries statistics and enforces regulations laid down by the Fisheries Regulation and shell fishing Regulation. The current ban on sharks, sea cucumber and shells will mean that the licenses it provides will have to be drastically curtailed. Enforcement of the WLPA (1972) provisions will be in the hands of the Forest Dept.

The Information, Publicity and Tourism (IP & T) Dept. sets tourism policy for the islands. It has built and maintains a number of tourist guesthouses, most notably in Port Blair, and at Cuthbert Bay and Kalipur. It has identified several areas in which tourism is to be expanded. Environmental concerns have to be in the forefront in choosing sites for tourism. As per the recommendations of Shekhar Singh Commission accepted by the Supreme Court, tourism in all forest areas has to be controlled and regulated by the Forest Department and no permanent/concrete infrastructure is to be created in forest areas for tourism.

Of special note here is the Master plan for Tourism prepared by the World Tourism Organization. This makes calculations of tourist carrying capacity based on water availability and the capability to treat sewage. The carrying capacity projected appears to be high and caution needs to be exercised before implementing any of this. Further studies are required and these are addressed later in this document.

This Department controls most of the non-forest land in the islands. These include the agricultural lands around the settlements. It also controls access to the Nicobar Islands, by means of administering a tribal areas permit system, as well as to all the tribal reserves.

The information, Publicity and Tourism (IP & T) Dept, sets tourism policy for the islands. Tourism is yet another priority sector identified for the economic development of the islands. Tourism will have effect on the utilization of the resources available in these islands and the accompanying pollution. Tourism in coastal and forest areas will have impact on the marine and forest ecosystems. Controlled development of tourism with no or low impact on the environment is called for.

The different settler groups that have been identified are:

Bengalis were brought in as settlers in the 1952-53, with Middle Andaman being used for settlement in the early 1950's and North Andaman around 1957-1959. After this, there has been a continuing influx especially over the last decade. These appear to be predominantly refugees from Bangladesh, and they have become rural farmers. Some of them have converted to fishing. Medicinal plants used are mainly ones brought by them from Bengal. Bengali settlements in Little Andaman happened between 1969-1974, and part of the Onge Reserve was denotified as a result of this.

This community has several components, mainly tribes from the Jharkhand and Chattisgarh regions. They were brought here before independence as forest labour. More arrived after 1948 to clear land for the new wave of settlers. They occupy mainly Government jobs. In rural areas they are concentrated around Baratang Island. They have developed rich ethno botany from the local plants.

These are mainly recent immigrants, and tend to come from the Ramnad area of Tamil Nadu. A number also moved here from Burma, where they had previously been settled. They are mainly urban dwellers, and form a significant part of the fishing community. They are also involved with business, transport, trading, contractors, construction labour, sand mining and road work.

An estimated 75% of the fishermen here belong to this community, and are from Nellore, Srikakulam and Vishakapatnam.

Refugees from Sri Lanka were settled here in the 1960's. There is a settlement growing rubber on Katchal Island in the Nicobars.

Karens were brought to the Andamans from Burma as forest labour in 1925. The community numbers 3000 totally, of which 600 live near Mayabunder. They are agriculturalists, fishermen, and work in Govt. Departments. Other communities have adopted their dug out canoes for fishing and transporting.

The Moplah community was brought here as convicts in the 1920's. Recently there has been an influx from other parts of Kerala. They are rice cultivators in North Andaman (Keralapuram) and in Middle Andaman (Betaur). A substantial number hold government jobs or are shopkeepers.

A large number of hotels have sprung up, especially in the last decade, to cater to the increased inflow of tourists. These range from small lodges to large resorts, ranging in quality up to 3-star status.

In urban areas, most of the smaller hotels are badly located and built, and lead to both congestion and the production of untreated effluents. In coastal areas there is pressure from business interests to relax the CRZ regulations to allow new complexes near the beaches. These are likely to lead to major environmental degradation if approved.

A lot of new businesses have come up in the islands over the last decade. A substantial number cater to the needs of tourists. These include travel agents, boat operators, tour guides, taxis, van and bus operators. They also include transport vehicle operators who depend substantially on tourism.

The different tribal groups are heavily dependent on natural resource use. The Nicobaris are dependent on fishing; the Andamanese, Jarawa, Onge, Sentinelese and Shompen are hunter gatherers. The resource use patterns of the different tribal groups are not understood and these need to be studied as a first step it any programme oriented towards their welfare.

These include domestic fishermen and foreign poachers. Information – both primary data as well as from other sources – is being gathered on type of catch, fishing areas, and quantities taken. A preliminary analysis shows that 10 shark fishermen account for over 240 tonnes of shark catch per year.

From the fishery point of view the indigeneous populations of ANI do not have a fishing community as such though they are known to catch fish for their own consumption. Fishing as a commercial activity is of a relatively recent origin. Fishermen from Andhra Pradesh, Kerala, Tamil Nadu and West Bengal have come to the islands through the settlement scheme of the Government or voluntarily. There are about 2256 fishermen families with a population of approximately over 11500. The population of active fishermen are around 2150.

Traditional craft, dinghies, and motorized and small-mechanized boats mainly carry out fishing. The fishing fleet of the Islands comprises of 1262 country crafts, 247 motorised and seven mechanical boats.

The Navy and Coast Guard play a major protective role in guarding against poaching by foreign vessels. In 2010 the Andaman and Nicobar Command was established and is a joint command for the defence services. This will lead to the induction of many more personnel into the islands and an increased infrastructure. Proper environmental planning has to be integrated into the expansion of this command to avoid degradation.

Bottom of Form

9

The Archaeological Background

Many recent scholars have done research on History of Andaman. The discovered Archaeological wealth here dates back the remains to 17th Century onwards. George Bebar in his book has refered about various rock sheltes. During the days of British as such no archaeological work was ever taken in this area. L. Sipriani has done some researches after independence upto 1949-54. He had published Anthropological research but his work on Archaeology remained unpublished. In the year 1970 P.C. Dutt published his research on Choldari midden. Thereafter Jarin Cooper excavated (1985-86) the choldari midden site. Jarin has explored around 43 shell midden site in the year 2002. In his exploration after every 2½ kms he could discover the mound containing shell midden sites. These sites were not very far from the sea and were situated in and around one km distance from sea. Archaeologists in 1910 and Cooper in 1980 excavated 2 choldari midden site and published his research. Hawa Mill of Andaman which was near to Batang Island (situated very close to caves) had some archaeologial remains, and this was even published. The chert tools which was discovered on the upper part of Andaman was published by Z. Cooper.

If we go in real sense to know the real meaning of kitchen midden, a trial excavation conducted by an Archaeologist

Dr. Phanikanta Mishra of Archaeological Survey of India, prehistory branch, Nagpur in 2002-2004 in South Andaman, Humpfreygunj was the first scientific research taken for the first time in a systematic manner. In two phases the habitational occupancy at this site was proved during excavation by these archaeological scientists. The broad explanation of kitchen midden in a lay language will be that for the "first time the mankinds foot was noticed near the sea on dry place." The river source was very close from this settlement. They had sufficient fish available for food. These settlers first came here as a temporary resident and thereafter from here they shifted to permanent resident. These mounds were camping ground for these settlers. Such temporary settlement mounds perished away in course of time due to sea waves etc. At many of the sites the Andamaneese stayed permanently. Their life was nomadic, hence at some places they could not stay for long.

The Archaeological exploration in Andaman is almost stopped by the present Archaeologists. The researchers avoid going to Andaman. Nigritos of Andaman is almost faded, whereas Andamans name comes to light. No work on Prehistory of Andaman has been done so far systematically. The discovery of Tools at this place is of Taolian era.

Archaeologists have established mankinds presence in Andaman from 2,280 years. Protohistorically if we see it seems that it is a very recent civilisation. The prehistoric discovery is yet to be completed. From where the Andamaneese came ? Where was their settlement before 2,280 years. Why they came in this year. Whether this Bay was shifted from some where or due to heavy terrains of the Bay all settlement was inundated. The Nagrito of this region Era (Phillipines), Mani (Thailand), Semang (Maleysia) are the remains of Nagrito Tribe. Whether the Andamaneese were the habitant here in this island since the beginning ? Whether from here they shifted to above places ? It seems that they had stayed here since beginning and around

8000 to 5000 before were habitants at Astronation (Malaya) Austroasiatic (Kheebar, Nicobari) and (Thai, Burma) in Sino Tibbet. It seems that at these places new tribes had occupied and thereafter they migrated here. It is very essential that a planned research is taken at this area. The vedodoid tribe of Srilanka is also very much similar to these tribe of Andaman and the DNA Test may confirm this.

Archaeologists from Archaeological Survey of India Prehistory Branch, Nagpur had excavated in South Andaman Humfreyganj an archaeological remains in 2002-2003 of the shell midden site. One mound of 35 metre in height and 30 metre in length was scientifically excavated. Some mounds were discovered in North East of this town. Archaeologists could find the shells here in abundance. Archaeologists have excavated the site stratigraphically. The earliest phase had Rocky layer and the remains of sea and above it was well of mud with floor. In this excavation archaeologists discovered hand made Pottery Pointed shells, Bones, Stone and the glass weapon were the remains discovered here during the excavation. The Potteries (20 cm) were noticed soon after 20 cm digging. The Potteries size in radius was around 13 cm × 9.5 cm and thickness was around 8 cm. The colour of these Potteries were Red or Chocolate. In some Pottery designs were also seen.

Besides this place the team of archaeologists explored, Dhanikhere, Muslim Basti (Orrabraj) Chauldari, Lohaberik (2 mounds) barathguda and trial trench was laid. Here the most of the sites had shellmidden remains.

In Andaman the first tribe came to light was the same as mentioned above. All had only one language. After the Britishers in 1858 this theory that one tribe build here was not found correct. Many other different tribes were noticed in this region. They had settled at various other mounds and had sheltered in this region. In the 'Tribal' settlement in this region it was also noticed that a big tribe settlement at one place with various spring had scattered all over the Island. In this settlement various other tribes also joined them. The independent tribe sometimes used to be friendly and at times they were quarelling with each other. Aryorto (on the sea coast) and Imataga (Forest tribe) were developing in this geographical scenario. It is learnt that for 10,000 years, they lived on flower, leafs and animals flesh. The main tribe was onge, Jarwa, Jangil and Senthili. The main power rested with onjos or onge tribe. This tribe was never separated in other tribes and they remained one. Till 1890 the scholars had done very less research and this was also noticed that many of these tribe perished because of Famine. In the past years some effect of Indian and British culture was also noticed on these tribes. They started marriage among various tribes. With these relations some affect of Indian Burwe and British was seen.

At present the tribes are very few and all this region is left virgin for the Archaeologists to do their research.

I

Appendix

The entire group of islands are fertile for study by the various groups of scholars associated with different subjects. Being an integral part of the country, these groups of islands make themselves distinguished from the rest of the country. Some special characteristics which can be noticed here are not found in the other part of the land. Port Blair is probably the only city in the country where rain water is used as drinking water. The entire groups of islands survives on HSD oil and power generation in the islands is negligible. Monkeys are known as vegetarian where as a group of monkeys living in Great Nicobar i.e. in Campbel Bay are crab eater. The administration works hard to save the flora and fauna of the islands. Hatching of tortoise eggs is encouraged. Crocodiles which are normally found in plain water are encroaching the sea sore. A variety of pigeon named as Andaman wood pigeon has been declared as state bird in Nicobar group of Island. Andaman Teal is local word which is found near the sea. Mega pode is state bird and is a rare species. A type of animal found in sea called dungong is a state bird.

The islands are having more than 450 varieties of medicinal plants and the local tribes are aware of the potency as well as utilities of these plants for different purposes.

Among the tribes 'sentinals 'are most hostile and not friendly. Nicobaris are literate and are in mainstream. They are in job and business as well. Jarwas were hostile earlier. Once during police firing a jarwa lad got his leg fractured. He was treated well in the hospital and there he could learn Hindi. After treatment when he retired to jungle, he conveyed the message that out side people are equally good. Jarwas also speak in Hindi. However, they use a few worlds only for communicating with each other. They are the only negroits tribe in India with deep black complexion. Till date they are living nacked but they are found of red materials. Normally they avoid killing the pregnant and newly born pig. They survive on honey and pig is their principal diet. Normally they take shelter where plenty of water is found. They continue to change ther places so that the natural resources of one place only is not exhausted.

The mangrove forests, running along the costline between high spring tide and mean sea level, around creeks, backwaters, and flat rocky shores, form a distinct barrier of vegetation that is the first peculiarity of the Andaman forests to hit the eye. Behind this first line of mangroves rises the next set of species, that thrives better in less saline water and greater stagnation, such as Bruguiera, Luminitzera, and Aegiceras.A third, distal, tier has the Nypa fruticans palm and such others as Avicennia, Heritiera, and Xylocarpus species.

Behind the mangroves, and on the edge o the sandy beaches, are the littoral forests, with the towering Mimusops littoralis, known as the mohwa, as the most recognizable species, with its long, deeply cracked, white-barked trunk and luxuriant shady crown.

In this zone are also the pandanus or screw- pine , known locally as 'bread fruit' , which form one of the local staples; and, wherever the soil is a dry marine alluvium, with carbonate and phosphate o lime, coconut palms. The last are native to the Nicobars, or at least seem to be, for no one among the tribals remembers a time when they were not growing.

These forests are impenetrable without a dao to hack a way through; and in Great Nicobar, where the riverine alluvium provides ample ground for their growth, they have effectively kept the interiors safe from intrusion. On hilltops that are fertile, with alluvial soil that has a relatively high degree of humus, occur the evergreen tropical forests. Here again the vegetation is abundant and luxurious, with a multi-storeyed canopy, but somewhat more irregular than in the case of the giant evergreen forests, and with an absence of shrubs below. On the lower reaches of the same hills that support evergreen on their tops, we find moist, deciduous trees , which shed their leaves, not in any one season but throughout the year, and which contribute the finest timber. The famous padauk is a deciduous tree, as are the white dhoop, the white chuglam, the black chuglam, and the papita.

The cumulative record, put together by botanists such as Colonel Kyd, Kurz, Prain, Parish, and Vasudeva Rao, so far extends to nearly 2000 different species of indigenous angiosperms, belonging to nearly 700 genera and 140 families, 14 per cent of them endemic; 500 exotic species; and nearly 100 fern species.

Another aspect of Andamanese flore generating some curiosity is the medicinal plants found in the Andamans. A large part of the knowledge on this aspect has been derived from the tribals , and the early convicts who came in contact with them before they, too, lost them to modern medicine. An interesting discovery, for example , is of the plants(orophae katschalia Kurz which the Onges use, and Amomum aculeatum Roxb. That the Jarwas do) whose juices have a tranquillizing effect on the honey bee, and makes honey collection a painless affair for both the collector and the bee. A list of medicinal plants so far identified can be found in Appendix II.

The work done by such zoologists as A. Alcock, W.T. Blanford, R.B.S. Sewell, B. K. Tikader, A.K. Das, N.V. Subba Rao, and scientists of the Zoological Survey of India, the National

Oceanographic Department and the Madras Crocodile Bank, has collated a great deal of valuable data. The marine fauna so far studied form a list 3757 species long, and may be divided into five categories of marine life - male fauna, phytoplanktons, algae, marine invertebrates, and vertebrates. Of these, the most interesting to the lay visitor to the Islands are the invertebrates and vertebrates; the corals, which have become the main tourist attraction of the Islands; the sea cucumbaers(trepang) or beche de mer, which attract poachers from South East Asia; the shell fish, for their attractive and unusual sea-shells; the huge clams, whose shell every householder on the Islands seems to use as a flower pot in his garden; the turtles, crocodiles, snakes, for the stories they contribute; and the legendary dugong, which few have seen but most have heard about. The last is the most intriguing. The dugong , also called the sea- cow, is 2 or 3 m in length, and considered an aquatic ungulate, with its tail evolved to help in swimming, body modified into a streamlined shape, and hind legs atrophied into extinction.

Elephants were first imported to work in the forests, and continue to be employed by the Forest Department till today. In 1968, some forty of them were abandoned and left on Interview Island by one of the timber companies that failed. Goats, introduced by the seafaring British, with the altruistic aim of providing meat for shipwrecked sailors, have been reported to have learned to drink saline water in a marvel of adaptability and proliferated to such numbers as to pose a real threat by their grazing, to the plant species on the Islands. As to the deer, the Forest Department, which at one time invoked the Wildlife (protection) Act, 1972, for their protection, has been controlling their number by periodically declaring them as vermin and allowing their hunting.

The reptilian population of the island forests is similarly placed. Of the 778 species of larger reptiles, comprising 4 species of turtles, 1 of crocodile, 32 of lizards, and 40 of snakes, 13 species of snakes and 10 of lizards are endemic; and 7 have been declared endangered (Appendix III). These are the estuarine crocodile, Andaman water monitor lizard, four species o turtles, and the python. The Andaman water monitor, or monitor lizard, shares its preference for fish, frogs, birds rats, and snakes with the crocodiles; lives near the same estuaries as the latter; and, at sizes of 2 to 2.5 m, provides good meat and skin.

Alone among all the reptile, it is the sea snakes that have escaped extermination, and that because of the speed with which they move and their reputation, justly earned, or being extremely poisonous.

The Islands are a bird watcher's paradise, and have so been considered since Blyth began making an ornithological record in 1845. He was followed by a long list of enthusiasts, including famous names Kurz, Prain, Walden, Allan Hume, Osmaston, Baden Kloss, and, in recent years, Humayun Abdul Ali and B.K. Takader. With its 270 species and subspecies of birds , fully 39 per cent of them endemic, the mystery of the origins of the islands deepens.

The administration of Andaman in the British period was in the hands of Superintendents from 1858 to 1871. Dr. James Patterson walker was the first Superintendent and the last Superintendent was major F.L. Playfair. Chief commissioner took over. Subsequently and Gen. sir Donald Martin Stewart became the first Chief Commissioner. The first Indian to become the Chief Commissioner was I. Majid ICS who took over from Mr. N.K. Paterson ICS in 1947. Sri S.C. Sharma IAS was the last Chief Commissioner and after the end of his tenure in 1982 Sri M.L. Kampani IAS became the first Lieutenant Governor of Andaman Nicobar Islands who joined in the year 1982.

Andaman Jail had a different code of conduct for the female convicts. They were divided into two classes first and second class. Second class convicts were subject to strict jail disciplines for three years they used to receive only food and clothes. Three year good conduct shall make them eligible for transfer to Ist class women in first class shall reside in barracks and work in sheds. They shall receive rations, clothings and a money allowance of 8 annas a month. Different types of restrictions were imposed on married and unmarried women so far as their interaction with outside world was concerned.

Women who prove refractory were liable to be transferred to punishment ward to have their task increased their hair cropped close and subject to close confinement.

A new culture emerged and the tradition of culture and the national feeling spread through out the area of the mainland found a new dimension in these confined islands standing as a symbol of mini India and as an appendix and the bibliography of the entire Indian philosophy and culture. People from different strata of society, caste and religion were transported to these Islands. They all were Indian and freedom fighters. These identified them and not the caste and religion and their geographical identities. It led to the foundation of Andaman society.

In a faithful application of its shrewd policy to divide and rule, the British government of India had drawn upon prisoners from all parts of the country to fill up the jail in the Andamans. Those who opted to stay back had nothing in common except a severing of their familial links, the stigma of being criminals, and the pain of becoming outcastes by their transportation across the seas. The census documents of 1901-31 reflect this diversity in the origins of the self supporters, and in their religion, caste and languages. In 1901, the self supporters were only 2859 in number, of a total penal colony population of 16,256, but comprised over 400 sub castes and castes, from more than thirteen states. They spoke altogether forty one languages, but as emple recorded, ' no doubt a philologist would discover a great many more'; professed every conceivable religion; and engaged in a vast variety of occupations.

A distinguishing feature of the colony was its lack of regard for caste barriers. The outstanding characteristic of the set was the grave deficiency in its number of women. Even before the settlement began, the need for convicts to have their wives with them had been noted as necessary for stability. It was, indeed, integral to the Stamford-Raffles system of reform:

While a convict remains unmarried and kept to daily labour very little confidence can be placed in him, and his services are rendered with so much tardiness and dissatisfaction that they are of little or no value; but he no sooner marries and forms a small settlement than he becomes a kind of colonist, and if allowed to follow his inclinations he seldom feels inclined to return to his native country.

Walker, as the first Superintendent , had even made elaborate arrangements to transport the families of twenty-five convicts under a secure escort to the Islands. But the fear among Hindus o becoming outcastes by crossing the seas and the ill repute of the Islands had both, worked against the scheme, and all uniformly declined. As we have seen , the government then hit upon the scheme of transporting women convicts to the Islands, beginning the traffic in 1860, and arranging marriages between male self supporters and female convicts on a ticket of leave, in order to stem the kind of immorality that is part of any all male establishment. But notwithstanding repeated inspections and several changes in the rules in this regard, some veering towards leniency and other to severity, and despite the women in general being amenable to marriage and the chance to settle down outside the prison in matrimony, their number in the colony remained woefully small.

A surprisingly large number of the women prisoners were widows incarcerated on charges of infanticide, the dupes of close male relatives and a closed and unforgiving society, and had no home or family to go back to. Marriage also meant a release ahead of time from the exacting routine of prison life, and the rest of the sentence spent in comparative security. The penal administration ensured a legal marriage. A self supporter was entitled to fee rations and free use of village servants for six months; free agricultural implements; an exemption from cess for the first three or four years; house sites, up a to 10 bighas of land on licence for cultivation; and Rs. 5 per month for a wife with an extra Rs. 2 per month for a child. In later years, when the expenditure on the settlement came under critical scrutiny, this was one area identified as requiring better supervision. Till as long as their husbands had not obtained their tickets of leave, and were in Port Blair, the women were assured security and a degree of comfort.

As far as the language of the Andaman in olden day concerned much is not known. The tribals who are the only originals of the islands use communicative words only. Nicobaris probably are the most advanced tribes and scholars have been able to collect the folk tales of the Car nicobaris. These tales are of special value for the folk lore students. In several cases they follow a track widely different from the usual legends. In their folk tales mother nature dominates and we find mention of sea, sky stars, coconut trees and coconuts. They have their own stories about the bats who according to their folk tales were human beings earlier, the sharks are the by-product of the cruelty of human being and that is why they attack the human being till today. There is also a story as to how the man became a python, how the Island of chowra was discovered, story of wild pigs and many other similar short stories are popular among the Nicobaris children.

Still in Andaman we find the so called 'locals' who are considered as permanent residents of these islands in addition to the tribes who are the only natives of these islands.

These islands are probably the only parts on the country where all festivals of India like Saraswati Puja, Durga Puja, Holi, Eid, Bakrid, Moharram, Vishwakarma Puja, Pongal, Onnam, Deepawali are celebrated with equal respect. Hindi is a language used throughout the nook and corner of Andaman. Caste is no bar and marriage is settled accordingly.

Now a days there is no dearth of quality schools & both private and run by Government. A chain of central schools are there besides school like Carmen, Blair and Vivekananda Vidyalaya is there. Higher education is run under the supervision of Chennai University.

II

Appendix

In the Andaman Islands more than 400 plants are found which are of medicinal value and are used in the treatment of various types of ailments. Besides the antipyretic plants, medicines are made for anthelimintic, anti-fertility and patients of astringent. These plants are useful too the patients of respiratory trouble, diabetes, dropsy, urinary trouble, epilepsy, eye disorders, fileria, liver disorder, leprosy, mumps, piles, gastrointestinal trouble, malarial and simple fever, Rheumatic pain, sexual disease, skin desease, snake bite, swellings, bone fractures, tooth ache and other diseases. (Source- Kiran Dhingra Gazetteer.)

Plants of Medical Value occurring in the Andaman and Nicobar Islands

Ailment/Disease	*Name of the plant*	*Family*
ANODYNE (ANTIPYRETIC)	Adenia penangiana (Don) de Wilde	Passifloraceae
	Adenostremma lavenia(L.) Kuntze	Asteraceae
	Blumea balsamifera(L) DC.	Asteraceae
	Cassia alata L.	Caesalpiniaceae

	Costus speciosus (koen) Sm	Costaceae
	Crateva religiosa Forst. f.	Capparidaceae
	Hedyotis biflora (L.) Lamk.	Rubiaceae
	Jatropha gossypifolia l.	Euphorbiaceae
	J. curcas L.	Euphorbiaceae
	Paedera scandens (Lour.) Pierre.	Fabaceae
	Pongamia pinnata (L.) Pierre.	Fabaceae
	Tacca leontopeta-loides(L.) Ktze	Taccaceae
ANTHELMINTIC	Aerva lanata Juss.	Amaranthaceae
	Barringtonia racemosa(L.) Roxb.	Lecythidiaceae
	Clerodendrum viscosum Vent	Verbenaceae
	Costus speciosus (Keon) Sm.	Costaceae
	Glycosmis arborea(Roxb.) DC	Rutaceae
	Merremia peltata (L.) Merr	Concolvulaceae
	Raulfia sumatrana L.	Apocynaceae

	Scindapsus officinalis(Roxb) Schott	Araceae
	Scoparia dulois L.	Scrophulariaceae
	Sida acuta Burm. f.	Malvaceae
ANTI-FERTILITY	Achyranthes aspera L.	Amaranthaceae
	Dioscorea bulbifera L.	Dioscoreacea
	Dioscorea pentaphylla L.	Dioscoreacea
	Erioglossum rubiginosum (Roxb.)Bl	Sapindaceae
ASTRINGENT	Ipomoea pescaprae (L.) Sweet Ssp. Brasiliensis (L.) Oost	Convolvulaceae
RESPIRATORY TROUBLE		
Asthma	Acanthus ilicifolius L.	Acanthaceae
Asthma	Acalypha indica L.	Euphorbiaceae
Asthma	Bacopa monnieri (L.) Penn	Scrophulariaceae
Cough	Barleria prionitis L.	Acanthaceae

Asthma	Barringtonia racemosa (L.) Roxb.	Lecythidiaceae
Cough	Blumea balsamifera (L.) DC.	Asteraceae
Asthma	Boerhaavia diffusa L.	Nyctaginaceae
Asthma	Costus speciosus (koen.) Sm	Costaceae
Asthma	Curculigo orchioides Gaertn	Hypoxidaceae
Asthma	Dioscorea pentaphylla L.	Dioscoreaceae
Cough	Dischidia major (vVahl.) Merr.	Asclepiadaceae
Cough	Dregia volubilis (L.f.) HK.f.	Asclepiadaceae
	Syzgium cuminii(L.) Skeels	Myrtaceae
	Tabernaemontana crispa Roxb.	Apocynaceae
	Tylophora indica (Burm.f.) Merr.	Asclepiadaceae
	Urena lobata L.	Malvaceae
	Weddelia biflora (L.) DC.	Assteraceae
DIABETES	Catharanthus roseus(L.) Schott	Apocynaceae

	Syzygium cuminii (L.) Skeels	Myrtaceae
DROPSY	Barleria prionitis L.	Acanthaceae
	Cassytha filiformis L.	Cassythaceae
	Elephantopus scaber L.	Asteraceae
DIURETIC (URINARY TROUBLE}	Achyranthes bidentata Bl.	Amaranthaceae
	Aerva lanata Juss	Amaranthaceae
	Anacardium occidentale L.	Anacardiaceae
	Bacopa monnieri (L.) Penn.	Scrophulariaceae
	Crateva religiosa Forst. f.	Capparaceae
	Curculigo orchioides Caertn.	Hypoxidaceae
	Dregia volubilis (L.f.) Hk.f.	Assclepiadaceae
	Hibiscus tiliaceus L.	Malvaceae
	Paederia scandens (Lour.) Merr.	Rubiaceae
	Pepromia pellucida H.B.K.	Piperaceae
	Phyla nodiflora (l.) Greene	Verbenaceae

	Phyllanthus urinaria L.	Euphorbiaceae
	Streblus asper Lour.	Moraceae
	Terminalia cataopa L.	Combretaceae
	Urena lobata L.	Malvaceae
	Vitex negundo L.	Verbenaceae
EARACHE	Acalypha indica L.	Euphorbiaceae
	Aerva lanata Juss.	Amaranthaceae
	Dischidia major (Vahl) Merr.	Asclepiadaceae
	Pongamia pinnata (L.) Pierre	Fabaceae
EMETIC	Calophyllum innophyllum L.	Burseraceae
	Dregia volubilis L.f.	Asclepiadaceae
	Paedera scandens (Lour.) Merr.	Rubiaceae
	Trichosanthes bracteata(Lamk.) Voigt	Cucurbitaceae
ANTI-EMETIC	Amaranthus spinosus L.	Amaranthaceae
	Macaranga indica Wt.	Euporbiaceae
	Sida acuta Burm.f.	malvaceae

EPILEPSY, FITS, AND HEADACHE	Achyranthes bidentata Bl.	Amaranthaceae
	Ardisia solanacea Roxb.	Ayrsinaceae
	Aristolochia tagala Cham.	Aristolochiaceae
	Bacopa monnieri (l.) Penn.	Scrophylariaceae
	Boerhaavia diffusa L.	Nyctaginaceae
	Calotropis gigantean (L.) R. Br.	Asclepiadaceae
	Clerodendrum viscosum Vent.	Verbenaceae
	Glycosmis arborea (Roxb.) DC.	Rutaceae
	Hernandia peltata Meissn.	Hernandiaceae
	Hyptis suaveolens (L.) Poit	lamiaceae
	Ipomeaa pescaprae (L.) Sweet	Convolvulaceae
	Raulfia sumatrana L.	Apocynaceae
	Vitex trifolia L.f.	Verbenaceae
	Weddelia biflora(L.) DC.	Asteraceae
EYE DISORDER	Agerratum coryzoides L.	Asteraceae

	Breynia retusa (Dens.) alston	Euphorbiaceae
	Calophyllum innoiphyllum L.	Burseraceae
	Dregia colubilis (L..) Hk.f.	Asclepiadaceae
	Globa marantina L.	Zingiberaceae
	Merremia Peltata (L.)	Convolvulaceae
	Scoparia dulcis L.	Scrophulariaceae
	Urena lobata L.	Msalvaceae
FILARIA	Eclipta prostrate (L.) L.	Asteraceae
	Elephantopus scaber L.	Asteraceae
LIVER DISORDER	Aphanamiixis polystachya (Wall.) Parker	Meliaceae
	Barringtonia racemosa (L.) Roxb	Lecythidiaceae
	Boerhaavia diffusa L.	Nyctaginaceae
	Caesalpinia bonduc (L.) Roxb.	Caesapiniaceae
	Eclipta prostrate (L.) L.	Asteraceae
	Glycosimis arborea (Roxb.) DC	Rutaceae

LEPROSY	Anacardium occidentale L.	Anacardiaceae
	Calotropis gigantean (L.) R. Br.	Asclepiadaceae
	Cynometra ramiflora L.	Caesalpiniaceae
	Hyptis suaveolens (L.) Poit	Lamiaceae
MMUMPS	Ardisia solancea Roxb.	Myrsinaceae
	Dischidia benghalensis coleb	ascepiadaceae
PILES	Ageratum conyzoides L.	Asteraceae
	Amaranthus spinosus L.	Amarabnthaceae
	Curculigo orchioides gaertn.	Hypoxidaceae
	Dioscorea bulbifera L.	Dioscoreaceae
	Homonia riparia Lour	Euphorbiaceae
	Mesua ferrea L.	Clusiaceae
	Paederia scandens (Lour) Merr.	Rubiaceae
	Phyllanthus virgatus Forst f.	euphorbiaceae

	Syzygium cuminii. (L.) skeels	Myrtaceae
GASTRO-INTESTINAL TROUBLE	Acanthus ilicifolius L.	Acanthaceae
	Acalypa indica L	Euphorbiaceae
	Aerva lanata Juss.	Amaranthaceae
	Amomum fenzlii kurz	Zingibera eae
	Ardisia solanacea Roxb.	Myrssinaceae
	Aristolochia tagala cham.	Aristolochiaceae
	Bacopa monnieri (L.) Penn.	Scrophulariaceae
	Barringtonia racemosa (L.) Roxb.	Lecythidiaceae
	Caesalpinia bonduc (L.) Roxb.	Caesalpiniaceae
	Cassytha filiformis L.	Clusiaceae
	Cordia grandis Roxb.	Euphorbiaceae
	Cycas rumphii Mig.	Hypoxidaceae
	Dioscorea bulbifera L.	Caesalpiniaceae
	Donax cannaeformis (Forst.) Schum	Dioscoreaceae

	Euphorbia hirta L.	Asteraceae
	Glycosmis arborea (roxb.) DC.	Rutaceae
	Hibiscus tiliaceaus L.	malvaceae
	Jatropha curcas L.	Euphorbiaceae
	Leea indica (Burm.f.) Merr.	Anacardiaceae
	Morinda citrifolia L.	Rubiaiaceae
	Ophiorrhiza mungos l.	Rubisaceae
	Pepromia pellucida H.B.K.	Piperaceae
	Raulfia sumatrana L.	Apocynaceae
	Streblus asper Lour.	Moraceae
	Urena lobata L.	Malvaceae
	Vitex negundo L.	Verbenaceae
	Zanthoxylum ovalifoplium Wt.	Rutaceae
MALARIAL FEVER AND FEVER	Aegle marmelos Corr.	Rutaceae
	Aerva lanata Juss	Amaranthaceae
	Amomum fenzlii kurz	Zingiberaceae
	Barleria prionitis l	Acanthaceae
	Coesalpinia bonduc (L.) Roxb.	Caesalpiniaceae

	Croton argyratus Bl.	Euphorbiaceae
	Homonia riparia Lour	Euphorbiaceae
	Raulfia sumatrana L.	Scrophulariaceae
	Vitex negundo L.	Verbenanacea
	Zanthoxylum ovalifolium Wt.	Rutaceae
RHEUMATIC PAIN	Amischotolype mollissima Hassk.	Commelinaceae
	Ardisia solanacea Roxb.	Myrsinaceae
	Barleria prionitis L.	Acanthaceae
	Coldenia procumbens L.	Clusiaceae
	Diosorea pentaphylla L.	Dioscoreaceae
	Elephantopus scaber L.	Asteraceae
	Lantana camara L.	Verbenaceae
	Urena lobata l.	Malvaceae
	Vitex trifolia L.f.	Verbenaceae
SEXUAL DISEASE		
Gonorrhoea	Amaranthusi spinosus L.	Amaranthaceae
Gonorrhoea	Calophyllum innophyllum L.	Clusiaceae

Gynaecological trouble	Donax cannaeformis (Forst.) Schum	Marantsaceae
Syphilis	Dioscorea bulbifera L.	Dioscoreaceae
SKIN DISEASE	Acalypha indica L.	Euphorbiaceae
	Ageratum conyzoides L.	Asteraceae
	Cassia alata L.	Caesalpiniaceae
	Dregia volubilis (L.f.) Hk.f.	Asclepiadaceae
	Euphorbia hirta L.	Euphorbiaceae
	Terminalia catappa L.	Combretaceae
SNAKEBITE (NICOBARESE)	Annona squamosa L. (Leaf – juice)	Annonaceae
	Datura metel L. (Leaf-paste)	Sollanaceae
	Parabaena sagitta Miers (Leaf-paste)	Menispermaceae
	Side acuta Burm. f. (Leaf-paste)	Mallvaceae
SWELLINGS/ BONE FRACTURE	Alstonia macrophylla G. Don	Apocynaceae
	Barleria prionitis l.	Acanthaceae
	Cassia alata L.	Caesalpiniaceae

	Dioscorea pentaphylla L.	Dioscoreaceae
	Eclipta prostrate (L.) L.	Asteraceae
	Jatropha curcas L.	Euphorbiaceae
	Mucuna gigantean (willd.) DC.	Fabaceae
	Thespesia populnea Correa	Malvaceae
	Vitex trifolia L.f.	Verbenaceae
TOOTHACHE/ GUM TROUBLE/ PYORRHOEA	Aristolochia tagala Cham.	Aristolochiaceae
	Barleria prionitis L.	Acanthaceae
	Claooxylon indicum Hassk.	Euphorbiaceae
	Elephantopus scaber L.	Asteraceae
	Jatropha curcas L.	Euphorbiaceae
	Lannea coromandelica (Houtt.) Merr.	Anacardiaceae
	Morinda citrifolia L.	Rubiaceae
	Spilanthes paniculata DC.	Asteraceae
	Streblus asper Lour.	Moraceae
	Symplocos racemosa Roxb.	Symplocaceae
	Zanthoxylum ovalifolium Wt.	Rutaceae

III

Appendix

The Effect of the Andaman Penal System

15. In considering the possible adoption of a remodelled Penel System for the Andamanas based on a fresh law, I would desire to explain how the existing System has grown up and how the adoption of such a proposal would affect the officials and the convicts subjects to its results.

16. As a preliminary observation, I would remark that the Prisons Act is strictly for prisons alone, and if it is to be applied to the Penal Settlement as a whole, then the result would be to turn the Settlement into a prison. Such a prison would cover an area officially of 473 square miles and actually of 327 square miles, containing grazing and arable lands, swamps, dense forests, large harbours and inlets of the sea, hill up to 1,500 feet, large and small villages, round which it would be impossible to place any artificial boundary, and it would be equally impossible to divide it up into ards or portions separated by artificial barriers, i.e., it would never he practicable to convert it into a prison such as in contemplated by the Prisons Act.

17. Andaman Penal System has all along grown up on its own lines independently of the Indian Prison System, and has never been based on the latter. The fundamental principles out

of which it has grown take their rise from and are still much more largely, than any one who is not a student of the system would suppose, imbued with the very first ideas ever evolved on the subject. The Andaman System is at root the former system of the Straits Settlements, thus. The first temporary Superintendent of the Andamans was Captain (afterwards General) Henry Man, who was generally instructed in January 1858 by the Government of India as to the treatment of the convicts and given his powers under the Mutineers Acts, XIV and XVII of 1857 (since repealed). General Man was trained in, and long Superintendent of, the Penal Settlements of the Straits. He was succeeded by Doctor J.P. Walker in March 1858, who drew up rules sanctioned by the Government of India and based on his instructions, which were identical with these given to General Man. These were followed by the Port Blair and Andamans Act XXVII of 1851 and by modifications of the rules by successive Superintendents and by Lord Napier of Magdala, as the result of an official inspection of the Settlement in 1863. In 1868 General Man became permanent Superintendent and embodied in the Andaman System the Straits Settlements Penal Regulations which he brought with him, and thus brought the System still more closely into line with that of the Straights Settlements. General Man's modifications still colour almost every part of the Andaman Manual. Sir Clive Bayley took General Man's rules and drafted out of them a formal Regulation in 1871. This draft was given to Sir Donald Stewart for comment by Lord Mayo, who took a great personal interest in the Andamans, and was subjected to the scrutiny of Mr. Scarlett Campbell in 1872 and of Sir Henry Norman in 1874, both formally deputed to inspect the Andamans, in consultation with Sir Donal Stewart, then Chief Commissioner and Superintendent. Their joint labours results in the Andaman and Nicobar Regulation, 1874, and in the Governor General in Council's Rules and the Chief Commissioner's Rules of the same year. In 1876 a new Andaman and Nicobar Regulation was drawn up, but the Rules under the

Regulation of 1874 were continued. It is these Rules *plus* the Superintendent's Bye-laws (Settlement Standing Orders) authorized thereby and modified from time to time by Government of India orders and by the Commission of Sir C.J. Lyall and Sir. A. Lethbridge in 1890, that form the still growing Andaman Penal System of the present day.

The Superintendent is right in saying that the Cellular Jail is primarily intended for the incarceration for six months of convicts on arrival, and secondly, for local bad characters.

In paragraph 8 of Messrs. Lyall and Lethbridge's Report on Port Blair, it was stated that they though it necessary that steps should be taken to increase the penel character of imprisonment in Port Blair during the earlier stages of a convict's detention, both in order that there might not be too great a disparity between the discipline in India and beyond seas, and also in order that the convict may be incited to lead a regular life in transportation by some experience of the severity of the preliminary stages to which a condemnation for misconduct will cause him to revert. In paragraph 12 it was recommended that, for a year or two, the preliminary stage of separate confinement in cells fox six months should be tried only with habituals or specially selected prisoners who have been sentenced for very serious crimes. It was propose that a Cellular Jail containing at least 600 cells should be constructed without delay; and it was observed that, when the system was found to work successfully, the number of cells could be gradually increased to meet all requirements, including the accommodation of prisoners now sentenced to the Chain-gang.

2. From what has been stated above it would seem that there is no objection to granting the permission sought in paragraph 3 of the Superintendent's letter, to fill the Cellular Jail, pending completion with the worst characters received by each batch from India and with selected local bad characters.

3. In paragraph 4 of his letter, the Superintendent says he understands that any kind of work may be given to prisoners incarcerated in the Cellular Jail, and that, if suitable labour is not forthcoming, giving them nothing to do will not be objectionable. He proposes, however, to give all the Cellular Jail prisoners occupation, and says he understands he is at liberty to find them any work suited to the jail conditions and to the wants of the Settlement.

Perhaps it may be said that these matters lie entirely within the Superintendent's discretion.

J.H.F., 17-4-95

F.W.W., 19-4-95.

To Secretary—The above seems right, but the Honourable Dr. Lethbridge might see.

L.M.T., 20-4-95

Major Template is proposing to do what it was arranged between him, Dr. Lethbridge, and myself that he should do. But I should like Dr. Lethbridge to see in case he has any further suggestion to make.

J.P.H. 22-4-95

PORT BLAIR—JUNE 1800

Report on the working of the Penal Settlement of Port Blair by C.J. Lyall and Surgeon Major A.S. LETHBRIDGE

From

C.J. Lyall, Esq., C.I.E.,

Bengal Civil Service

and

Surgeon-Major A.s. Lethibridge, M.D.

Inspector General of Jails, Bengal

To

The SECRETARY To the Government of India,

Home Department

Dated : Calcutta, the 20th April 1890

Sir,

In accordance with the instructions contained in your letters No. 7, dated 6th January, and No. 80, dated 15th Junaru 1890, we visited the Penal Settlement at Port Blair, and conferred with the Superintendent in regard to the points mentioned n your letters and such other matters constructed with the working of the Settlement as the limited time at our disposal enabled as to discuss.

In Appendix A annexed to this report will be found a diary of our proceedings, showing the steps taken to obtain information on all points which we found it neessary to require into. We were fortunate in bring able before leaving Calcutta to visit the Alipure and Presidency Jails with Colonel Cadell, and in having him as a fellow passenger on board the S.S. Peshwa.

Before proceeding with our report, we desire to express our acknowledgements to Colonel Cadell for the excellent arrangements he is kindly made to show us over the whole

Settlement and to obtain for us all the information we required. The Medical Officer in charge, Dr. G.P. Mackenzie, was unfortunately incapitate by sicness from accompanying us on our inspections of the hospitals and other sanitary arrangements and we were unable to discuss with him the improvements which suggested themselves in the course of our enquiries.

2. Preference of Convicts for transportation as compared with imprisonment in Indian jails—The first to which our enquiry was directd was the statement made in the Report on Jail Administration in India which is quoted in full in paragraph 2 of your letter of the 15th January. As Jail, we had a good opportunity for testing the correctness of the statement that prisoners preferred transportation to Port Blair to imprisonment in Indian jails. Accompanied by Colonl Cadell, we visited the Alipore Jail and saw about 120 prisoners who were to be despatched on the following day to Port Blair. Besides these persons, we had paraded for our inspection a large number of old and deerepit transportation prisoners who had been finally rejected by the Medical Committee and were therefore undergoing their sentences in the Alipore Jail. There was among the prisoners a Sikh convict who had recently escaped from Port Blair and had been re-captured. Without a single exception both those who were about to start for the Andamans and those who had been rejecte expressed a desire to be transported though he knew that stripes and the chain gang awaited him at Port Blair.

PORT BLAIR—JUNE 1800

Home Department Proceedings, February, 1893

Preposed construction of tramways from the Aberdeen Jetty to the site of the Cellular Jail and at Minne Bay Brick field.

Agrreably to the orders contained in paragraph 7 of your letter No. 867, dated 17th October last, regarding the proposed Cellular Jail at Port Blair, I have the honour in submit the following estimates and plans regarding the necessary tramways:

(1) Report and estimate of tramway from Aberdeen Jetty to the site of the building.

(2) Report and estimate of tramway at Minnie Bay

(3) Site Plan of Cellular Jail.

(4) Site of Brick-making station, Minnie Bay.

(5) Section of main road from Aberdeen Jetty to the site of the Jail, and section of road from jetty to kilns, etc., at Minnie Bay.

(6) Illustration of Hauling Engine.

(7) Messers, John Fowler and Co.'s Catalogue.

2. It will be seen that I am submitting a proposal for a tramway at Minnie Bay where hte bricks will have to be made. it is with reluctance that I have had to add this second tramway, but without it, I fear, there will be great delay in making the bricks. Even with the help there will be unusual difficulties once the work is fairly started in getting a continuous supply of bricks, so that the work is not checked or hindered for months for what of them. The actual brick-making season can only last a few months, i.e., from 1st January to May, but the other processes connected with it, such as getting the clay, cutting the firewood, etc., etc., I will try and carry on all through the year, and with

the help of this tramway this may be possible, but without it the supply of bricks will run short. We are now very hard up. We are now some six hundred men short of the number available this time two years ago. As soon as the season for the transport of convicts comes to an end, our number will have decreased much more owing to releases, deaths, and other causes. It is therefore very necessary to have all the materials on the spot to go on with brick-making as fast as possible during the season.

3. The land on which the clay and jungle are now will eventually, when cleared, become available for the Navy Bay Ten Garden, with but comparatively little extra labour. I should mention this not as an argument for aloowing us this tramway now, but to show that when the clay and jungle have been removed this land will become available for a Government industry.

4. I am very anxious to keep down expenditure on this jail, and I am very certain the best way of doing so, in actual money, will be to make our preliminary arrangements, which unfortunately must cost cash money, as complete as we can, so that when work.

References

1.	Tourism in Andaman & Nicobar Islands	Dr. N Rajavel
2.	Andaman and Nicobar Islands union territory, Tourism & Biodiversity effect on the ecosystem of the islands & strategy and action plan	RSC Jaivaj and HV Andrews
3.	Andaman and Nicobar Islands	RVR Murthy
4.	Andaman long back in 1863	Frederic J. Mout
5.	Gazetteer	Kiran Dhingra
6.	"Unsung Heros of freedom struggle in Andaman 'who's who.'	Rashida Iqubal.
7.	Wikipedia	

PLATES

1. The Jarwa Child (Courtesy Gazetteer)

2. The Jarwas (Courtesy Gazetteer)

3. Aerial view of the Island

4. Another view of the Island

5. Aerial view of the Sea

6. Another view of the Sea

7. View of Sea

8. Khuradera Beach Andaman

9. Another view of Khuradera Beach Andaman

10. Sea Shore of Wandoor

11. Another View of Wandoor

12. A Sketch of Nicobar Ship

13. A view of the Island after Tsunami

14. Cellular Jail Port Blair

15. Port Blair Jetty

16. Prisoners in side the Cellular Jail

17. Ross and smith Islands Diglipur

18. Ross Island

19. View of Sunset in Andaman

20. View of the floating Island

21. View of the Island

22. View of the Sea from the Hill